HOW
NOT
TO
Manage
People

HOW

NOT

TO

Manage
People

*The leadership mistakes keeping
your team from greatness*

HarperCollins
Leadership

An Imprint of HarperCollins

Published by HarperCollins Leadership, an imprint of HarperCollins Focus LLC.

Published in association with Kevin Anderson & Associates: https://www.kawriting.com/.

Book design by Aubrey Khan, Neuwirth & Associates.

ISBN 978-1-4002-1852-3 (eBook)
ISBN 978-1-4002-1843-1 (HC)

Library of Congress Control Number: 2020936142

Printed in the United States of America
20 21 22 23 LSC 10 9 8 7 6 5 4 3 2 1

Contents

Section 2

It's All about Communication

Section 3

It's All about Leadership

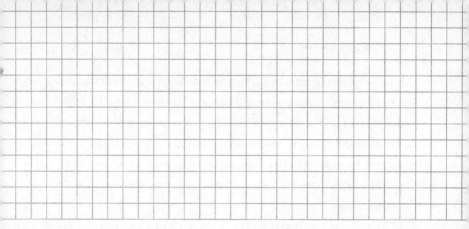

Introduction

Managers everywhere are f***ing it up. Ask anyone if they have ever worked for a terrible manager, and they will likely say, "Why yes, yes, I have. Let me tell you about this one nutjob I worked for a few years ago," or "Yes, my coworkers and I used to joke that we were going to take a cue from *Horrible Bosses* or *9 to 5* and make our manager's 'untimely' death look like an accident."

People, it seems, are more than willing to share their personal manager horror stories. Indeed, the stories that make up the body of this book are a testament to a desire to expose poor management practices. They are about real managers and the very real mistakes they make. These stories will make you laugh or cringe and wonder how awful managers such as these held down jobs in the first place, let alone secured management positions. You may recognize some examples of poor management behavior because your boss demonstrates or inflicts them upon you, or maybe, if you are honest, you yourself have demonstrated some of them from time to time. If, in fact, the latter is the case, fear not! All is not lost. There is still time to turn things around.

I myself have had the displeasure of working for more than a few bad managers throughout my career. There's the sales manager, for example, who insisted I drive 200 miles to meet with him at the corporate head office on my first day working for the company as a sales rep. I walked into his office, fully expecting an orientation session, and instead received a weak "welcome to the company" speech and some basic administrative instructions, before he handed me a Rolodex (this was many years ago), pointed to a blank wall, and said, "Those are your accounts, north is that way," before turning back to his work. A five-hour round trip and I was in his office for less than 40 minutes. It was my first day with the company, and as I drove back north, the only thing I knew for certain was that I was going to look for another job.

Interestingly, he features later in a "how-not-to" story; spoiler—he's the guy that fell out of one of his sales rep's cars and almost got run over (I wasn't the rep, but I have to admit, the story made me smile).

Being a manager, however, is not always easy. Whether you are working for someone else or running your own business, there are hundreds of things you can mess up every day, even if you are trying your best to be a good manager. One size doesn't fit all, every person is different, and every situation is different. It's certainly easier to fall into bad habits and be a poor manager than it is to strive every day to be a manager and leader who is looked up to by all those who report to them.

To complicate things, we have three distinct social groups who have differing views of how companies should be run. Boomers are the primary residents of corporate C-suites across America, Gen Xers are waiting their turn, and following behind are the very different generational group, the millennials, who are increasingly inhabiting middle-management positions. Much has been written about the differences between these groups, especially millennials, but these groups have more in common than one might think.

Millennials communicate differently because they often prefer to send a quick text rather than pick up the telephone. They also tend to dress more casually, have a more relaxed attitude about work hours, hold work-life balance in high regard, and are far more flexible around where and when a job gets done. Little of this, however, has any bearing on what makes a good manager and a good leader. Good management, moreover, transcends the age of the manager.

Great managers of all ages share a few key traits: integrity and fairness, adaptability, accountability, and empathy. They are strong communicators and leaders, they inspire and empower those around them, and they learn from their mistakes. Great managers know that there are always opportunities for improvement, and each day they strive to be better shift leaders, supervisors, middle managers, directors, or CEOs than they were the day before.

Get the management part of corporate life right and the rewards are significant. Get it wrong and you will see profits evaporate like a mirage in the desert, along with a promising career and advancement.

Complacency often leads us to believe our personal or our company's management practices are good, or at least good enough, but

Mental Health America's "2019 Mind the Workplace" survey found that over 50 percent of those surveyed said they were unmotivated at work and would not recommend their workplace to anyone else.[1] Only about half of respondents said they got enough direction to perform their work effectively. One of the most damning findings, not to mention a costly one for employers, was that almost 60 percent of those surveyed were currently looking for a new job.

One of the biggest things a good manager or leader can do is to inspire confidence in those they manage. Mental Health America, however, found 80 percent strongly agreed that their company's culture made them feel less confident about their work performance.

The "how-not-to-win-manager-of-the-year" stories in this book will hopefully encourage you to take a long look at your management techniques and style and work toward becoming a better manager; this will not only benefit your employees, it will have a significant impact on your bottom line. They are all true stories and real examples; however, in many cases, the names of those involved, the type of organization, and the geographical location have been changed to protect both the innocent and the guilty. I have also combined some stories where managers acted in very similar ways, as this allowed me to provide a broader perspective on the management challenge under discussion.

Poor, bad, and downright horrendous management is alive and well and living in your town, probably in your company. Hopefully, the tales of hopeless and helpless managers in these pages will help you become a better manager and, potentially, win that manager of the year award.

It's All about the Team

One certain way not to get nominated for manager of the year, let alone win the award, is to begin to believe your own press. Managers who think they know it all—and who fail to understand that they don't have to be the most knowledgeable person in the room, just the best manager and leader—can be a real danger to their department or their company. A little humility goes a long way when it comes to managing people. In this chapter, we'll take a look at some people who mistakenly thought it was all about them.

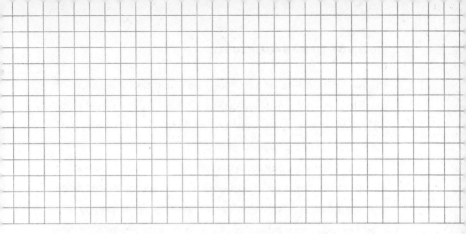

ONE

It's All about You,
Not the Team

DAWSON WAS PROMOTED above other, more worthy, candidates, in part at least because he had attended an Ivy League school. His feeling of entitlement was well ingrained by the time he became head of sales. His first priority when he took over as sales director was to complain about his office chair; he headed down to purchasing to order one that was bigger, better, and more ergonomically fitting to his new stature—or at least his large ego! His second priority was to see if there was a better office with a nicer view that he might relocate to before he moved in his business awards and the large number of business books he owned (but had only ever skimmed). Dawson was also proud of how fit he was and would cycle into work each day, propping his bike against the wall of his office. Unfortunately, he would also change out of his designer, figure-hugging cycling clothes in a tiny closet (with no real door) in his glass-walled office, in full view of several staff members . . . but that's another story.

It was a full week before he managed to get around to meeting his sales team. In the meeting room sat five eager, optimistic faces and several others, who after taking one look at the preppy way their new boss dressed and his smug look, were significantly less hopeful. Dawson didn't disappoint the latter group. He spent twenty minutes telling his team how perfect he was for the job, how well he had done in his previous job, and how he was going to turn this "ramshackle sales department" into the shining star of the company. All this before he had formally introduced himself and discovered anything about the people he was supposed to be leading—even their names.

By the end of the meeting, Dawson had failed to create a connection between himself and his team. He either didn't know or couldn't remember everyone's names and didn't bother to learn which territories they represented. Dawson, however, was oblivious to his shortcomings and patted himself on the back for what he felt was a good initial meeting. He was sure that his team members were all highly motivated to have such an experienced person leading the department and that increased sales would quickly follow.

Unfortunately for Dawson, sales did not increase. What did increase, however, was employee turnover, and after two short weeks in his new role, Dawson received his first letter of resignation (the first of many, as it happens). To Dawson's dismay, it was one of the senior salespeople, Jodie, and she was the company's number one performer. Jodie had often been approached by the company's competitors but had never been interested in leaving. That was, until the new head of sales was hired. Now, leaving the company seemed much more appealing than coming in to work each day and watching Dawson strut around and preen himself like some rooster in a hen house. He was arrogant and self-serving to say the least, and it was apparent to Jodie that he didn't actually care about the team. She had seen his type before: Managers like Dawson who used the team to make themselves look better. Managers who were solely interested in their own success, and who didn't realize the importance and value of their team.

Dawson made the common mistake of getting wrapped up in his own immediate success; he felt good about his promotion and wanted to shout it from the rooftops. One of the first things he did was announce it on Facebook and LinkedIn and then eagerly awaited the congratulations that followed. He bought champagne, the real stuff, and took it home to his wife. He called his brother and sister and his mom and dad and reveled in the glory of achievement. Not once, in the early days, did he consider the team he was about to manage.

Less than two weeks later he was fighting his first fire—Jodie's resignation. His boss wanted to know why the devil their best sales rep was leaving and demanded to know what Dawson had said to her to make her leave.

Dawson, of course, was dumbfounded; he was a great boss, why would she leave? He could have understood if that short guy with the unruly hair—what was his name—had left, the one that worked the Southwest . . . or was it the Southeast?

THAT IS THE challenge; sometimes bad managers don't know they are bad managers. That's because they see the word *manage*, not *lead* in their title. How could Dawson have handled things a little better? First, he could have shown a little humility when he got the promotion rather than thinking, "Well, it's about time." Thinking you are entitled to a job, a promotion, or almost anything in life is going to get you into trouble at some point. Rather than think only about what it meant to him to become the head of a department, he should have thought about what it meant to the team he was about to lead, and the company. The hiring team had entrusted him with a ton of responsibility and talent, but all he could see was the current and potential glory.

Let's go back to that first meeting and see how he could have handled things better. In fact, we should go way back to when he first accepted the job; at that point he should have gone to the HR department and requested his team's employment files and studied them. After all, he was being entrusted with their future success. Who were these people? Where did they come from? What jobs had they held in the past? How long had they been with the company? Had any of them had any issues with his predecessor? What did their last performance review reveal?

At the same time, he should have been studying his predecessor's files and discovering which team member managed which territory, what their sales targets were and whether they were reaching them, and whether they had received any training, either in-house, external, or out in the field. Dawson had been more interested in thinking about whether he'd get a corner office with a view and what bottle of champagne would most impress his wife.

If Dawson had been half the manager he thought he was, he would have walked into that first meeting with his sales team and told them that he was there for them and that his job was to support them in achieving their best potential; that this was a team effort and together they could achieve great things. He would have already known their names and their territories and would have made a point of going around the table and letting each person talk a little about their territory, their challenges, and their aspirations. He would have then followed up by asking everyone to tell him one thing that he could do to help them be more successful. In this way, the meeting would have become about them, not him.

If you are thinking, it's tough to put ten names to ten faces, here's a trick. At your first team meeting draw a rectangle depicting the table and a square for each chair. Then, during the roundtable introductions, write each name into the relevant square. Later, you will be able to imagine the faces around the table and refer to the name in the appropriate seat on your drawing.

> ∨ *If you are thinking, it's tough to put ten names to ten*
> ∨ *faces, here's a trick. At your first team meeting draw a*
> ∨ *rectangle depicting the table and a square for each*
> ∨ *chair. Then, during the roundtable introductions, write*
> ∨ *each name into the relevant square. Later, you will be*
> ∨ *able to imagine the faces around the table and refer to*
> ∨ *the name in the appropriate seat on your drawing.*

You may have noted that in the second (and much improved) scenario above, Dawson never talks about himself. When you take over a team, unless it is an abnormally fast appointment or replacement, you can bet the team knows all about you; they will have discussed you, Facebooked you, asked other managers about you—they'll know you by your reputation. The only question is, can you gain their respect because of, or in spite of, that knowledge?

How Not to Manage People

- Humility is for the undeserving; revel in your success.
- Status is important; negotiate, or take, that corner office, you earned it.
- Hang and place your awards and certificates prominently. That marathon certificate will be sure to impress, and it'll look good next to your degreesonline.com graduation certificate.
- Ensure every member of your team knows how well-qualified you are and how lucky they are to have you as their leader.
- Ignore any dissent among the ranks, they'll get over it. A few naysayers are irrelevant.
- Don't go to all the hassle of learning your team's names or anything about them in advance, you'll get to know them over time. The important thing is for them to know your name.

TWO

Your Number One Priority Is to Ensure the Team Makes You Look Good

t's surprising how many managers fail to recognize the value of their team and simply use their employees to further their own agenda. If only they could see that they would climb the corporate ladder far faster by basing their own success on that of their team.

CATHY WORKS AT an international advertising agency and is proud to be the youngest person ever to be promoted to vice president. She is certain that all she needs to do to become the first female senior vice president is to make her division the most successful in the company. Her rise to vice president had been quick and was based on her handling of—maybe taming is a better word—a particularly difficult major client that the company had been in danger of losing. In reality, her management experience was extremely limited—something she would have been wise to realize and try to rectify before starting her new job.

Cathy was good at reading people and she knew how to motivate them; she was friendly, outgoing, supportive, and always looked busy. She attended dozens of meetings, and in terms of corporate politics, was always in the right place at the right time. She had a wonderful talent for spotting people who were doers—those people in any team who make things happen, the top achievers. Unfortunately, she herself was only an achiever once removed; she motivated others to do great things for which she could take credit.

Cathy was Machiavellian; on the face of it she came across as an effective manager and a good leader and she managed to sustain that image—for a while at least. Outwardly she was highly supportive of her employees. She would bring them donuts and other treats on a regular basis and frequently compliment their work. She led with an almost too-light hand, but for the most part was there when a member of her team needed guidance. By and large she was well-liked and respected. Her underlying motives, however, were debatable. Above all, she was lazy. Her number one goal was to be seen by her superiors as the brains of her team—the person who actually made everything happen with everyone else playing minor, supporting roles.

By cleverly managing workloads she would ensure that her team members worked late on days when she knew her boss was also staying late. If a member of her team had something successful to report, she would always personally make the report to her boss, or the board, and minimize her team member's role in the project. She rarely allowed a team member to present anything unless it happened to be too technical for her and, even then, she would minimize their exposure to the people she was constantly trying to impress, often interrupting them when she felt safe, with the material being presented. On one occasion she actually put her hand in front of the face of one of her senior staff so she could interrupt and take over the presentation, a move that didn't go unnoticed by anyone present.

Cathy's plan worked for a period, but gradually her team became demotivated. It always seemed that they did all the work and she took all the glory. The quality of their work dropped off over time, mistakes were made, people resigned, and the team became imbalanced and ineffective. With fewer opportunities for which to take credit, Cathy started down another road that would lead her further away from that manager of the year award: she started blaming her team for her department's lackluster performance.

OFTEN, MANAGERS LIKE Cathy don't start out to manipulate; on that first day when they meet their new team, they may have the very best of intentions, but insecurity is insidious; it infiltrates the psyche like a musical earworm, always playing in the background.

People like Cathy have often never been formally taught managerial or leadership techniques; rather, they have worked their way up the corporate ladder by being in the right place at the right time, excelling in some particular area, or as a result of favoritism or even nepotism. They are basically winging it, and when people wing it, they fall back on their base instincts for survival and that, in terms of people management, is usually neither pretty nor effective.

If one day you realize you might be turning into a Cathy, or if you are being put into a similar situation, try to understand that a good manager and a good leader doesn't need to take the credit for every-thing. (We'll talk more about the blame game in Chapter Six.) Too many managers misunderstand their success goals; they think that what is important to their job is every small success along the way, when in fact the real goal is the success of the team and every member of the team. Help your team become successful and you will achieve departmental or divisional success. When your team is firing on all cylinders, and being noticed by management, they may appear to be in the spotlight, but the glow of corporate success is fully yours. Stand back, show humility, and watch the accolades pour in while allowing your team their moment of glory.

How Not to Manage People

- Employees are there to be used; the secret is to treat them well, get them on your side, and use them to further your career.
- Be nice to your team—bring them coffee and cookies. That way they'll be easier to manipulate.
- Ensure your subordinates work late and are visible when you know your superiors or other department heads are working late; it's all a matter of one-upmanship.
- Never let a team member present anything; it's your project, your glory. Interrupt them if necessary.

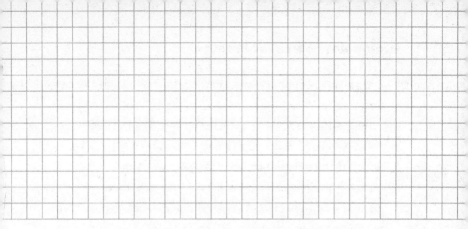

THREE

Information Is Power: Keep Your Team on a Need-to-Know Basis

DANIEL, A PROJECT manager at a management consulting firm, was lead consultant on a project for one of the company's biggest clients. His team was three weeks into writing an extensive environmental report when his boss, Justin, texted him to inform him that there was a major shift in deliverables: the contract with the client needed to be renegotiated. Daniel was thrown for a loop by the news. His team had spent a great amount of time working with the client to identify the key points the report needed to cover, even flying out to their offices on the West Coast, and they were now working on the table of contents and report outline. Daniel immediately texted his boss back to ask, "So do we stop work on everything then? No point even working on the outline until we have a new contract and know the new deliverables."

His boss replied, "We're doing the outline." This left Daniel confused. Should he continue as if nothing had changed? So, he replied, "If the deliverables are changing, won't that affect the outline?" Justin's quick reply didn't help matters, "I'll be in touch." Not to be brushed off lightly, Daniel shot back another text, "I'm not happy having my team continue with the TOC and outline before the contract is renegotiated and we have a clear idea of what the client wants." To which Justin replied, "Sorry I said anything."

Daniel by now was getting frustrated and said, "You needed to. I need to be in the loop." Justin's reply, below, characterizes the problem faced by many people working with a boss who is highly selective about what information he or she shares with their subordinates, "It's not worth it if you question and worry like this. I don't have time to go into all the details—it will be fine, trust me."

DANIEL WAS LAST seen by his team slowly banging his head against his office door. Justin's final words, ". . . trust me," epitomized Daniel's issue. Obviously, Justin didn't trust Daniel, but he wanted Daniel to trust him. Trust has to be earned and, in this case, Justin didn't reach the bar Daniel set for earning that trust.

Whether Justin was playing power games with knowledge is debatable; he may have wanted initially to share the new information with Daniel but became concerned that Daniel might take things into his own hands and contact the client directly. It may have been that Justin believed, like mushrooms, people grow better in the dark. It could even have been that Justin texted before he put his brain into gear and that it would have been better to first think through how best to communicate the news to Daniel and his team.

So, how could Justin have handled the situation better? Information is, without question, power: if you know more about any situation than someone else, you have greater control. But, ask yourself, could you have even more control and even more power if you were less secretive? First, Justin should have rationalized his fears, which were almost certainly:

- If I tell Daniel the whole story, he'll get upset and concerned about the future of the project and then he'll get stressed and that will lead to more questions and I don't have time to deal with all that shit.
- I don't want him getting involved. It's my job to deal with the client—that's my role.
- He'll demand more time, more people, a bigger budget, and I don't want to deal with that right now.

Justin's fears may seem real, but do they hold up to scrutiny? The first one is rational, but surely Justin wants Daniel to be invested in his projects, to care—doesn't he? And, in the end, it's Justin's responsibility to deal with that shit. Second, Daniel is the one working intimately with the client so Justin might have been better to include, rather than exclude, him from the negotiations. Daniel's insights, along with those of his team, might have been invaluable in understanding the impact of the new deliverables. Finally, if the project's deliverables were going to be modified significantly, it would be reasonable for Daniel to want to discuss changes in resources and budget. The big question is, wouldn't it be better to do that before renegotiating with the client, rather than setting a budget and expectations on which it might be difficult or impossible to deliver?

> ∨ *Good management technique is logical, but we as*
> ∨ *humans are often illogical and often self-defeating.*

Good management technique is logical, but we as humans are often illogical and often self-defeating. Justin ended up causing himself more problems in the long run than if he had been more inclusive from the outset. There is a point, of course, where some information has to be privileged, but in most cases, it's the tip of a very large iceberg. The more information you share, the less people imagine and, remember, it is human nature for people to imagine the worst. It is ironic that some managers withhold information as a form of control, to maintain power if you like, but in reality, by sharing it a little more they would gain greater control over outcomes.

> ∨ *The more information you share, the less people*
> ∨ *imagine and, remember, it is human nature for people*
> ∨ *to imagine the worst. It is ironic that some managers*
> ∨ *withhold information as a form of control, to maintain*
> ∨ *power if you like, but in reality, by sharing it a little*
> ∨ *more they would gain greater control over outcomes.*

In Justin's case, he did eventually renegotiate the contract, but in the process demotivated and alienated Daniel and his team. He also quite likely undermined Daniel in the eyes of the client; after all, Justin had initially promoted Daniel as being highly experienced and the right person for the job but then sidelined him during renegotiations when the project details changed.

How Not to Manage People

- People work best if you treat them like mushrooms—keep them in the dark.
- Team members should be kept on a need-to-know basis: the less they know the better.
- Knowledge is true power. Keep as much of it to yourself as possible and when necessary dole it out like candy to starving children. It'll make you look good and make them both happy and dependent.
- Don't trust anyone with more details than is absolutely necessary. After all, you are the manager, you don't need their help.
- Team members are far too needy; keep them on a tight leash so they become dependent on you.

FOUR

Ignore Feedback from Your Team—You Know Best

In the previous example, had Justin involved Daniel and his team to a greater extent he could have gained a tremendous amount of insight into the client and the client's project needs prior to entering into renegotiations. Also, it's quite likely the team would have been able to identify more efficient ways to assist the client with their new deliverables. Good managers listen to their teams and don't run roughshod over anyone's input. To quote an old cliché, there's no "I" in team.

JACK WAS A senior member of a team coding a custom system for a document management project. The project was late and full of bugs; it was off the rails and had been rejected by users. One member of the team suggested to the project manager that the best course of action would be to put the work on hold for a few days, bring everyone together to figure out what was going on, clearly identify the issues, find solutions, and then prioritize workload before continuing. There were many vigorous nods around the table. The project manager, however, looked the employee in the eye and said, "But that means we're paying the developers NOT to work. We can't have that. The project is already late, they just need to work harder."

BEFORE WE ANALYZE the story above, let's hear from Timothy Wiedman, a retired associate professor of management and human resources at Doane College in Nebraska. He has a how-not-to-manage story from when he was a young man working in the hospitality industry. It's about a rogue regional manager and other senior corporate executives who ignored him completely, with disastrous consequences.

IN THE MID 1970s, a decade before landing my first academic position, I was the general manager at a company-owned fast-food restaurant, which was part of chain. It enjoyed the second-highest volume in a three-state region known as the "Michigan District." During my tenure, sales volume had more than doubled. In addition to managing the restaurant, I also supervised on-the-job training for new salaried managers within our district. This led to the corporate vice-president of operations choosing me to conduct a month-long retraining program in California and

Arizona, where the company had reacquired previously franchised locations.

Before leaving I put my top assistant manager—one of very few female assistant managers in those days—Peg in charge. I trusted her to run the restaurant smoothly in my absence, which she did for a few weeks. Unfortunately, without consulting me or involving me in any way, my regional manager transferred her to another location to help solve a personnel issue he himself had created. There I was on company business in Phoenix and without soliciting any feedback from me he replaced Peg with my next most-senior assistant manager.

The first I heard of it was when I connected with the relatively inexperienced young man during my twice-weekly morning phone call to the restaurant. It was a bombshell; I was 2,000 miles away but could immediately tell by the tone of his voice that he was in way over his head trying to run such a high-volume location. I immediately called Peg and got the whole story: she was on the verge of tears telling me that the regional manager had told her that I wanted her to move on. I told her this was certainly not the case and asked her if she wanted to come back. Without hesitation she answered, "Absolutely, boss!"

I still had two weeks left of my training stint, so I told her that I'd do my best to fix things as soon as I was able. I did everything I could think of to get Peg back. I was diplomatic at first but when that got me nowhere, I raised a ruckus and went over my boss's head. Surprisingly, his superiors supported what I considered his underhanded actions.

Over the previous eighteen months, I'd been saving as much money as I could, to allow myself to eventually go back and finish college and subsequently graduate school. I had been close to completing my bachelor's degree when I'd been offered the position at the restaurant. Now, my relationship with my direct superior was severely strained and any respect I had for him had disappeared. At best I considered him only semi-competent. So, I decided, after weighing the pros and cons, to resign and return to school and become a full-time student. I gave thirty-days' notice; my boss was furious because few managers in the district had sufficient experience to manage my location's volume of customers. He told me, however, that he'd have my replacement within two weeks. Thirteen days later he dropped by unannounced, asked for my keys, and watched closely as I removed my personal possessions from my office. As I left, I recognized the new manager waiting in my boss's car. I seriously doubted he had the necessary experience, but I gave him the benefit of the doubt.

Several months later a general manager from the restaurant chain called me; he'd been one of my first management trainees. He told me that my nemesis had been fired, my old restaurant's sales volume had dropped by 32 percent, and apparently the termination had been very messy. Truthfully, I didn't feel much; I'd moved on, was doing quite well in college, and had no intention of ever looking back.

IN OUR FIRST story, Jack witnessed a typical management response, which is "I know best," or the blind faith, illogical answer, "We haven't got time to find a way to do it right, just do it!" Managers who have this attitude treat their team like slaves rather than colleagues. Treating people as valuable assets is vital to good management and good leadership. As a manager, you have to recognize that you are also a leader; the two roles go hand-in-hand. Everyone on your team is presumably there for a reason and brings something to the table—a skill, knowledge, a new perspective.

> ∨ *Treating people as valuable assets is vital to good*
> ∨ *management and good leadership. As a manager, you*
> ∨ *have to recognize that you are also a leader; the two*
> ∨ *roles go hand-in-hand.*

Think about it: In what possible scenario or world are additional ideas and perspectives a bad thing? Even silly ideas have their place in that they can stimulate conversation, provide some levity, or inspire creativity. Managers who believe they know everything, or believe they always know best, will always eventually crash and burn just as Timothy's regional manager did in our second story.

The most beneficial thing about encouraging and listening to feedback is that it shows you value your employees' opinions and respect their experience, knowledge, and skills. That is a major motivator and will inspire greater commitment, drive higher quality feedback, and more successful projects—projects in which you as the manager will share success.

> ∨ *Encourage employees to take greater ownership*
> ∨ *in what they do and the projects they work on.*

Encourage employees to take greater ownership in what they do and the projects they work on. Managers often don't realize that encouraging feedback and delegating more project ownership actually makes their job easier. Encouraging feedback and allowing a sense of ownership is rewarded by greater loyalty and respect. People in this type of environment will work additional hours and they will go out on a limb for you—they will go the extra mile. It's those people who can make departments and companies successful and turn managers into heroes.

As soon as you think you know it all, or that only you know best, you are on a slippery slope to unemployment or bankruptcy.

How Not to Manage People

- If team members knew anything worthwhile, they'd be the boss. Unilaterally making all key decisions is good management.
- There's no value in team feedback; it just muddies the water.
- Team members are more motivated when they have a strong dictatorial manager who doesn't need to rely on their feedback.

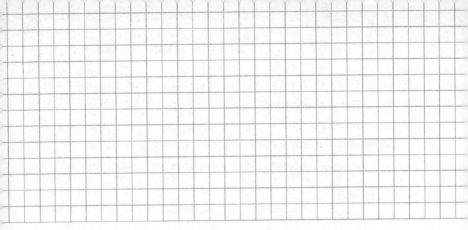

FIVE

Keep Control—Don't Empower Your Team

Empowerment is a gift to some managers and a curse to others. In the right hands, however, it can offer huge benefits. Before we discuss those benefits, let's hear a humorous (if it wasn't so awful) story about lack of empowerment. This happened to me, Mike Wicks, some fourteen years ago and shows how frustrating it can be both for customers and employees when management will not empower frontline staff.

I'D SPENT SEVERAL days working with the economic development director of a town in southern British Columbia, Canada, on their community profile and managed to wrap everything up earlier than anticipated. My flight from Calgary didn't leave until around 4 p.m. the following day, but I decided to drive to Calgary International Airport early the next morning in the hope that I might be able to get on an earlier flight. I'd been in the same situation several weeks earlier and the airline agent had put me on an earlier flight at no charge. On this occasion, however, I was flying a different airline because I couldn't get flights with my airline of choice. I arrived at the check-in counter some six hours early and asked whether there were any earlier flights. The late-middle-aged desk clerk smiled, said yes there were several, and asked for my ticket. As I had booked late, it was a full fare ticket, so I didn't anticipate any issues, especially as I'd been through the same experience recently with the airline's competitor. It all went downhill from that point; I was told that I would have to wait for my assigned flight.

I asked whether all the earlier flights were full and was told, "Not at all, in fact, I could get you on a half-empty direct flight leaving in thirty minutes." I looked blankly at him, waiting for the "but" . . . and wasn't disappointed. A ton of frustration erupted from the guy as he told me why he couldn't help me: "If you'd been here a few weeks ago, I could have changed your flight myself easily and seen you on your way as another satisfied customer. But the company has taken away our discretionary powers; never in my thirty years with the company have I been so exasperated and felt so unfulfilled. In fact, I'm here to tell you that XYZ Airline doesn't give a damn about you; it simply doesn't care anymore."

As I sat waiting for my flight, for a very long time, watching flight after flight take off for my destination with empty seats, I vowed I'd never fly that airline again. For the next two years, I had to visit my client in B.C. and fly through the Calgary airport almost monthly, but I never flew that airline again and told dozens of people my story. I felt sorry for the poor desk agent who could no longer do his job effectively and had to deal with angry passengers all day. I look back fondly on my days flying with my regular airline, where a flight change was as simple as checking whether there were any seats available on an earlier flight.

TIMES MAY HAVE changed—airlines today charge for any alteration to your flight—but the principles of empowerment remain the same. The first airline's policy of empowering its staff to allow changes where there was availability made customers happy and made its employees' jobs easier. The second frustrated both desk agents and customers.

The question is: Why then did airline number two introduce a policy that seemed to be counterproductive? Why, in fact, don't all employers empower their employees? If only life was that simple.

There are several reasons employers dislike empowering their team members. One centers around a lack of trust; that is, if an employee makes an error of judgment, it'll cost the company money. Another is a simple control issue, an inability to let go of decision-making, which is a form of power. Many are suspicious of customers trying to get something for nothing and taking advantage of good-natured employees. One genuine concern, often overlooked by managers, is that empowering employees can be difficult unless strict parameters are put in place. The danger lies in one employee making one decision and another making a different one in the same situation. This can confuse and anger customers. Let's revisit the airline story. If, as I sat at the gate, I started talking to a fellow passenger, and she told me she had managed to get on an earlier flight, how would that have made me feel about the airline? Even worse than before, right? This can happen when one person abides strictly by the rules and another interprets them differently. That's where training and the introduction of strict rules and parameters relating to empowerment are so important.

One positive aspect of empowering your team is that it frees up both you and them to do your own jobs. There is an element of delegation in empowerment but, remember, just because you delegate doesn't necessarily mean you are also empowering. When people are empowered, they tend to take ownership of their role and their responsibilities, and when they do that, they are less likely to abuse any power bestowed on them by the empowerment. In a team environment, it fosters a spirit of shared responsibility, collaboration, common goals, and allows a team to self-direct in an environment of trust. As a result, people are encouraged to fully utilize their skills and experience, share ideas, and seek answers to challenges. This, in turn, provides fertile ground for a broader perspective on issues and brings greater creativity to projects.

Empowering your team will ultimately mean less unnecessary interruptions for you as the manager. If all that sounds wonderful, but you are wondering how you leap into the empowerment abyss, the first thing you need to do is set your own ego aside. Trust your team; sure, give them guidance and training, set parameters, guidelines and such, but at the end of the day, leave them to it—resist the urge to micromanage.

> ∨ *Trust your team; sure, give them guidance and*
> ∨ *training, set parameters, guidelines and such, but at*
> ∨ *the end of the day, leave them to it—resist the urge*
> ∨ *to micromanage.*

How can you reach the point where you trust your team? By inviting team members into strategic discussions and sharing your vision, goals, and objectives. The more they understand where you are going and how you are going to get there (the road map), the more likely they are to keep on the right track. Of course, as with all empowerment, you will need to set generous boundaries, push people a little beyond their comfort zones, and then give them space and permission to grow. Allow the team and individuals to have input on their targets. Nothing is more demotivating than an impossible-to-reach target, so agree on targets that are aggressive but attainable.

Once you've empowered your team, or individual employees, congratulate them when they do good work. Remember that you have empowered them and, by so doing, you have given them additional responsibility. Poor managers mistake empowering people for dumping responsibility on them so they can take the blame when things fail. When mistakes are made, and they will be, don't chastise or throw a tantrum; help the team or individual learn from the situation.

Finally, mentoring those you empower will significantly increase your chances of success. If you don't include some degree of mentorship, you are basically setting stretch goals and then casting them adrift in a sea of responsibility. Check back in with them and discuss how things are going and see where you can help them succeed.

Remember, empowerment should be a natural process; leaders who think empowerment will turn a difficult employee, or department, into a successful one overnight will be sorely disappointed.

How Not to Manage People

- Empower your team—then it's their fault when everything goes wrong.
- Don't empower people. They'll make mistakes and it will cost the company money and you'll have to put everything back in order. Best to keep total control, it's safer that way.
- Empowering people is dangerous; people might do the job better than you. Best to keep all decision-making to yourself.
- Empowering people is too difficult; Paula's too soft and Brad's too hard ass. They'd treat customers differently. Avoid it—you'd have to create policy and boundaries and stuff, and that's too much like hard work.
- Customers are always trying to take advantage of your business. If you empower your employees, they'll give away the farm. Better to deal with any tough situation yourself, even if it takes you away from more important work.
- Ensure your team knows that you not only have the power to empower them, but also the power to take it back. You are a supreme being within your company.

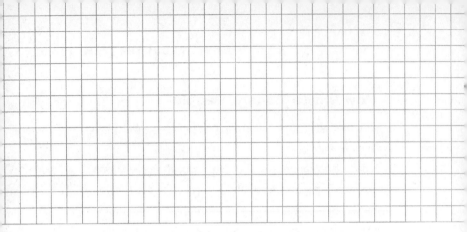

SIX

Don't Try to Find a Solution— Find Someone to Blame!

This is a common "How Not to Manage People" syndrome. Managers and business owners become so busy and stressed managing their operations, they lose sight of being a leader. They fall into the trap of looking outward rather than inward and resort to blaming anyone and anything for whatever goes wrong. To be clear, there is no upside to the blame game; it's a never-ending spiral to the bottom and creates more problems while solving absolutely nothing. When you blame others, you go blind to every other possible option or outcome. As Gloria Steinem said, "It's easier to blame the person with less power."[1]

GEORGE OWNS A manufacturing company in Texas that builds and installs custom high-end kitchens, home libraries, and bars. His clients are a mix of new homeowners who have taken a chunk of equity out of the sale of their previous property and wealthy people looking to give their homes a high-end refit. His clients don't hesitate to pay for quality but expect creativity and superior craftsmanship. This means he has to continually source expensive materials like hardwoods and high-end fittings. His tools are also state-of-the-art, and his table saws are fitted with SawStop to prevent injuries—when the blade detects human flesh, it stops in less than five milliseconds and the blade drops away. Having this safety device means, if one of his workers slips, they might get a tiny nick on their finger or hand, rather than losing an appendage altogether.

Mistakes, George realizes, are extremely costly. The people he hires need to be meticulous and skilled in working on custom pieces. A large project with the wrong finish, size, or error in construction has a huge impact on his bottom line, as he may have to redo the entire project, incurring the loss of time and wages involved. And that SawStop? Every time it activates, it costs George $250 for a new blade and the high-pressure cartridge that activates the process. Mistakes are costly.

George is extremely skilled and talented at his craft and, as a result, has high expectations of excellence from his team. He comes across as demanding and when employees make mistakes, George is furious. As a result of this behavior, employee turnover is high, which ends up costing more in both time and money in the long run. George has been known to complain that you can't find a person "to do the damn job properly these days!" He eventually comes to the realization that he needs help, so he hires HR consultant Jonathon. Let's hear the rest of the story from Jonathon.

George's biggest problem was the way he was handling his workers; morale and productivity were down as nobody knew who was going to get blamed next. Most of his employees were experienced but accidents happen even to skilled workers. I asked George how much training and supervision he gave his team and if he made an effort to balance any criticism with appreciation for work well done and provide ongoing positive feedback. I emphasized that positive feedback motivates people, and what a difference it would make to their performance if he could change tack and support his workers rather than discourage them. I was surprised at how much my suggestions angered George, even more so when I talked about offering perks to attract and retain experienced, skilled workers. I thought he was going to burst a blood vessel. He ranted for a while about how tough the industry was, how cheap his clients were, and how nobody understood the pressure he was under having to deal with the imbeciles who worked for him who were supposed to be damn craftspeople. He shouted, "I pay them a good wage, that's enough! That's all the bonus they need."

JONATHON WALKED AWAY with little hope that his recommendations on how to solve George's problems would be heeded. George had blamed his team, his industry, his clients, and now his consultant, for not understanding "how the world works." Until George is willing to change his old-school mindset, he will continue to run into the same problems.

For a while, Jonathon kept a watch on the company to see how it was doing. Unsurprisingly, George's HR issues gradually became unmanageable and his company eventually closed its doors for good. There are many Georges in businesses across the country;

they are focused on blame rather than solutions. If George had brought his team together and identified what training or assistance they needed, he could have helped them become more productive and better at their jobs. That, in turn, would have resulted in fewer mistakes. What he failed to recognize was that staff turnover was costing him significantly more than occasional, albeit frustrating, mistakes on projects.

> ∨ *There are many Georges in businesses across the*
> ∨ *country; they are focused on blame rather than*
> ∨ *solutions. . . . What he failed to recognize was that*
> ∨ *staff turnover was costing him significantly more than*
> ∨ *occasional, albeit frustrating, mistakes on projects.*

How Not to Manage People

- It's always someone else's fault; you can't get decent people anymore.
- You don't have time to train people or treat them like children—they need to grow up and do the damn job.
- Why give employees perks? You pay them, don't you?
- People shouldn't make mistakes, period. If they do, just fire them and hire better workers.
- Your job would be great if it weren't for idiot workers, customers, and all the other stuff that gets in the way of you doing your job properly.
- If anything goes wrong, blame it on the weakest link in your team. Protect yourself at all costs.

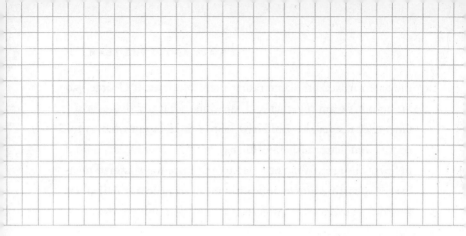

SEVEN

Play Favorites—
Reward the People You Like

Imagine working in an environment where the manager is selective about which team members he or she asks out for after-hours drinks. If you are one of the chosen few, it might not seem that bad, but if you happen to be one of those left behind, you can't be blamed for feeling resentful.

Managers who act in this way often do so to reward those people who are willing to work late or weekends when the manager is up against a tight deadline. The problem is that other excellent workers who have children or aging parents to look after are ostracized, not just when it comes to a glass of wine after work, but also when bonuses are handed out and promotions awarded. You might think that those who work the hardest should get those rewards, but from a management standpoint, it can cause problems over time when qualified people become disillusioned and leave. Working long hours should not be the only consideration when determining the value of team members.

Here's a story about a new manager falling into the trap of favoritism. It happened quite a few years ago, and again, we've changed both the manager's name, type of organization, and the area of the country where she worked.

JANET WAS GENERAL manager for a large business association in the southern United States. She was promoted to her new position from within the organization because she had some supervisory experience and was generally well-liked. Initially, both the board and her subordinates were excited about her appointment and had high hopes for the association's future under her management.

Unfortunately, after a few months, things started to sour a little and cracks began to appear in her management style. It became obvious to all concerned that she was favoring certain employees. It was small things at first; she would be friendlier and chat more with certain people. Others would be allowed to take longer breaks and receive extra sick days when everyone knew they were either not sick or were fit to return to work. She was tougher on some people for poor performance, and it became clear that there was a clique that could do no wrong; other members of the team, however, were held to higher standards and treated very differently. The latter group received veiled threats of termination and were bullied by Janet. Then there were those who fell into neither group and, under this social pressure, were virtually forced to align themselves with one side or the other. It didn't take long before the organization's staff was split into two almost equal halves. Some people saw the injustice and sided with those who were being mistreated and others realized the benefit of getting on Janet's good side.

Within six months, the atmosphere in the office changed dramatically; there were hushed whispers, covert meetings, and gossip—a whole lot of gossip. The association's real work suffered. Staff meetings were stilted, unfriendly, and people were wary about what to say and to whom. As we discussed in Chapter Six, blame became a currency and it was hurled back and forth between the two factions, and especially by Janet. Tensions mounted and were growing while Janet was oblivious to the climate she had created. From her perspective, the people she confided in were good, hard workers who were performing at a high level and helping her reach her organizational and administrative goals. On the other hand, the troublemakers (as she saw them) needed micromanaging to keep them focused and in line to ensure they did their job to her satisfaction. She couldn't understand why some of her staff decided to support these people, but they too were quickly becoming an irritant.

Poor management can take time to affect (or infect) an organization or a team; it doesn't happen overnight. During this time, Janet had been assuring the board that she had everything in hand, so it was years before the board realized that the association's operation was falling apart at the seams, and only then because several staff members approached the board about the situation. The litany of problems included several people taking stress leave and the resignation of three key people. This led to obvious understaffing and extreme workloads. Membership started falling and there was an overall erosion of confidence in the association from the wider community, including local government funders. In turn, this led to increasing numbers of mistakes, higher levels of stress, internal bad feeling, arguments, and a downward spiral into inefficiency.

Janet's board launched a formal investigation into the situation, hiring an HR consultant to interview staff. The final report was damning; it showed a complete breakdown in the team dynamic, trust from all sides was at an all-time low, and morale was all but nonexistent. The result was high levels of stress, rampant absenteeism, poor work quality, and, ultimately, significant loss of revenue.

The board interviewed Janet and began to see how her management style and personality played a major role in destroying what had once been a vibrant, effective team. She was dismissed and an interim management team was brought in to put the association back on track. It took more than a year for the team to recover from Janet's favoritism and to learn to trust one another again and become a cohesive unit.

FAVORITISM IS A very common problem among managers. It is a human trait to like some people better than others, and that's okay in our personal lives, just not in business. In business you need to keep an objective view as to the value of every member of your team. A key point to remember is that you don't have to like someone for them to be a valuable employee. And just because you like someone doesn't mean they are necessarily good for your company.

Another area where managers often fail is that they place a higher value on loyalty than experience or skill. Anthony Babbitt, a business consultant from Sioux Falls, tells the story of a company president who regularly fired qualified people only to replace them with less qualified people who were friends. That company is currently skirting bankruptcy and experiencing massive losses due to fraud. The problem is that once people realize that all you care about is loyalty, they learn how to fake it; true loyalty can often be when someone tells you something you don't necessarily want to hear.

> ∨ *The problem is that once people realize that all*
> ∨ *you care about is loyalty, they learn how to fake it;*
> ∨ *true loyalty can often be when someone tells you*
> ∨ *something you don't necessarily want to hear.*

How Not to Manage People

- It's only natural to have favorites among your staff; the other losers will understand.
- Take your best workers and the ones you like out for drinks after work; it'll motivate them to work even harder for you and inspire other employees to try to get into your good book. Win-win!
- Give bonuses and promotions to those who work the longest hours regardless of their skill or experience. People with children or aging parents to look after wouldn't be able to handle more responsibility anyway.
- Competition for your good favor is good for team spirit. It keeps people on their toes.
- Loyalty is always more important than skill or experience. That's why hiring friends is such a good idea.

EIGHT

Make Examples of People— It's a Good Warning to the Rest

There are many ways to motivate people, but embarrassing them in front of their colleagues is one that rarely works, especially if it involves yelling and screaming. Some managers are hot-blooded and naturally yell and others are more calculated and coldly use shouting at people as a form of intimidation.

Others single out people and make an example of them as a warning to the rest of the team. There is a story about Jim Pattison, the Canadian business magnate, who in his early career as manager of a car lot is said to have fired the salespeople with the lowest sales every month. In a 2016 interview, he denied ever doing it, but said he agreed with the principle. There is little doubt that such a practice would motivate people not to be in last place, but the demotivation of those salespeople inhabiting the bottom third of the pack would most likely outweigh the benefits in the long term. Here is a story from a manager who worked with a company director whose reputation and fiery temperament preceded her.

I WORKED CLOSELY with Arianna for a few years; at the time I was a divisional head and she was a director of the company. She wasn't my boss, but she was senior to me. In fact, she ended up becoming CEO, but that was some time after I left the company. At the time of this story, we worked in different departments but often our projects overlapped. I remember she used to erupt from her office if she discovered someone had done something wrong and scream at the person in front of the whole department. Her staff consisted of almost all young women (this was typical of the industry at the time) and I'd often turn up and see the aftermath of "Tropical Storm Arianna." Boxes of tissues were a fixture on every desk. In the early days, I thought she was the ultimate harridan but then one day she turned her wrath on me just outside her office door. She harangued me about something or other for what seemed like minutes but was probably less than 20 seconds.

By this time, I knew her well and I couldn't help it—I just laughed and said, "Oh, come on, Arianna, you don't mean any of that," and walked into her office. She looked at me with thunder in her eyes and said, "Aargh, it doesn't work on you," and then she smiled. Arianna was disliked by many of her staff and turnover in her department was high, but those like me who saw through her façade ended up liking and even respecting her. Over the years, she softened and when the company was bought out by a massive international corporation, she eventually became CEO of its entire European operation.

IN THE STORY above, Arianna was one of those people who had difficulty controlling her emotions and took her frustrations out on her staff. She was not a bad person, or even a bad manager, but she was misguided with regard to her management technique. She was somewhat of a legend in her industry and young people felt privileged to work with her and therefore stuck it out far longer than others in a similar situation might.

In the end, Arianna was successful. But at what cost? Could she have achieved the same level of success by being a little more human? Of course she could, but in the end her way of managing was far less damaging than a manager who uses the "break them down to build them back up" method of management. These managers believe making examples of people will motivate both them and other team members and do so in a calculated manner.

The problem with any form of berating people or making examples of them is that it causes stress, which doesn't make people better at their jobs, nor does it make them more intelligent. In fact, it has a negative effect on their cognitive functioning. Managers who act in this way may well see employees working harder, trying to be better, but in the end they are less effective at their jobs. If you ask managers who act this way if they believe employee engagement is a positive thing, most would say yes, but then these same people yell at team members, which only results in distancing them from management.

Which cadre are most likely to be more motivated and work harder—employees who like and respect their boss or those that dislike or fear them? If you believe it is the latter then you might want to review your costs relating to hiring, firing, and retraining employees.

Managers who treat employees poorly and who call them out in front of their colleagues are the same ones who are slow to give recognition for good work while doling out criticism for short-comings at every opportunity. They instill fear, threaten job security, actively play the blame game, show a lack of compassion, and thrive on unpredictability. They rule over a negative work environment that exudes stress and anxiety. That is *How Not to Manage People* in a nutshell.

> ⌄ *Which cadre are most likely to be more motivated*
> ⌄ *and work harder—employees who like and respect their*
> ⌄ *boss or those that dislike or fear them? If you believe*
> ⌄ *it is the latter then you might want to review your costs*
> ⌄ *relating to hiring, firing, and retraining employees.*

How Not to Manage People

- A great way to motivate people is to shout at them in front of their colleagues; it will teach them to do better next time.
- Berating team members makes them want to please you, so productivity and accuracy increases.
- Threatening job security for underperforming team members is a strong motivational technique.
- Making an example of an idiot on your team doesn't demotivate the rest of the team, it just puts them on notice.
- Treating people badly on occasion is just part of a manager's job.
- Being hard on people makes them better at their jobs; you're really doing them a favor.
- Shouting at people is a positive form of employee engagement.

NINE

How to Use Passive Aggressiveness to Make Your Team Feel Bad, Scared, and Mad—and Resent You

Mention to friends that you have a passive-aggressive boss and you'll have everyone nodding in agreement; it seems that the workplace is a common location where one can witness first-hand this aberrant behavior.

If you are unsure how to recognize passive-aggressive behavior in yourself, here are a few indicators that might mean you are one of THOSE bosses. Do you limit access to information? Do you play one employee against another? Do you ignore team members that have annoyed you, or give people the silent treatment? Do you praise people one moment, only to ream them out the next? Do you purposefully withhold praise? Are you, or would people call you, overly controlling? Do you evade conflict by saying things like, "I hear what you are saying, Bill, but you don't know the whole story and if you did, you'd see things a lot differently," and then refuse to share the relevant information that would give Bill the complete picture? Are you persistently indecisive? Finally, do you take credit for the work of other people?

> ∨ *Passive-aggressive managers are a virus in the*
> ∨ *workplace; their actions lead to stress, depression,*
> ∨ *bullying, and a massive drop in overall morale.*

Passive-aggressive managers are a virus in the workplace; their actions lead to stress, depression, bullying, and a massive drop in overall morale. This results in excessively high staff turnover, which is extremely costly. Mental Health America's *2019 Mind the Workplace* report found that 62 percent of employees felt the culture in their workplace made them less confident in their performance and 66 percent said that workplace stress negatively affected their sleep.[1]

Here is a great example of passive-aggressive behavior from Ron Carucci, managing partner of Navalent, an organizational and leadership consulting firm, and bestselling author of *Rising to Power: The Journey of Exceptional Executives*.[2]

JEFF WAS A new supervisor of a ten-person claims processing team for a mid-sized insurance company. The company had recently implemented a scheduling system that awarded the best shifts to the most productive claims reps. In Darwinian fashion, reps who underperformed in any given month, including through circumstances outside their control, were in danger of being relegated to shifts that forced them to miss their kids' soccer games or make last-minute changes to personal plans.

Following in the company's Darwinian footsteps, Jeff felt the best way to preserve his omnipotence was to drop not-so-subtle reminders around his reps about how a misstep could land them the graveyard shift. He'd say things like, "Hmmm, looks like someone is vying for a few late nights next week, huh?" Of course, the team resented the new system and the sacrifices it forced on them. As a newer supervisor, Jeff had relatively thin skin, so he overpersonalized any expression of discontent.

When Lindsey came to him and asked for an exception to her shift assignment so she could attend her daughter's spring concert, Jeff feigned sympathy: "Gosh, it really will suck to miss that concert. I guess next month you'll double down on your quota a bit harder, won't you? I'm so sorry about this time." To avoid being a complete jerk, however, he agreed to check with someone else on the team to see if they'd be willing to switch shifts with Lindsey. But instead of making a direct and sincere appeal, he showed up in the break room when three of his reps were there and manipulatively complained, "I cannot believe the nerve of Lindsey—coming into my office and whining about missing her daughter's spring concert next week! Honestly, after the rest of you worked so hard to hit your numbers last month, she had the gall to want me to make an exception just for her. But don't worry, I didn't sell any of you out."

Jeff knew full well what would happen next. Kristy, also a mom, piped right in: "Well, gosh, Lindsey switched a shift for me a few months back. If it would help, I'd be happy to switch with her. Those of us who are parents know these moments are hard to miss. Let her know that I'll cover for her." Of course, Jeff had to have the last word. "Oh, you don't have to do that, Kristy—that's more than I could ask of you. But, okay, well, if you really insist, I'll let Lindsey know that she owes you big-time." As the door closed behind him, the three reps in the break room rolled their eyes at Jeff's pathetically transparent manipulation.

Jeff went right to Lindsey's cubicle and in a cold, stern voice said, "Lindsey, can you please come into my office?" Naturally, Lindsey was terrified that she was getting fired and that's exactly what Jeff wanted her to think. When she entered his office, he was standing and continued with his somber tone, "Would you please close the door and sit down?" When she sat, so did Jeff. He folded his hands on his desk, exhaled, and said, "Well, I have some good news for you, and I hope you appreciate this. I had to go out on a limb for this, but I was able to convince Kristy to switch shifts with you next week so you can go to your kid's concert. I hope you won't make a habit of this, and I hope you know how fortunate you are to be part of such a wonderful team."

Lindsey left feeling relieved but also guilty. She went right to Kristy to thank her, who dismissed her grateful exclamations with, "Hon, it's no big deal. Don't give that creep's immature crap a second thought. You enjoy that concert. Karma's a bitch, and he'll get his one day."

WHILE READING A story like this may make your skin crawl, there are managers like Jeff everywhere. Some are more subtle in their manipulation while others are even crueler. In his immaturity and inexperience, Jeff missed numerous opportunities to reinforce great team behavior and engender loyalty to him as a leader and to the clients they served, despite the company's deployment of a scheduling system that promoted self-serving behavior.

Instead of feeling insecure about his power or colluding with the team's frustration over the new system, Jeff could have listened empathetically and engaged his team in a productive conversation centered on how best to make the system work for everyone in spite of its limitations.

Instead of guilt-tripping Lindsey into feeling bad about asking for time with her family, Jeff should have taken a radically different approach. He should have separated any conversation surrounding her performance at work from the conversation about her desire to attend her daughter's concert. By connecting the two, Jeff sent mixed messages and promoted an exploitive culture. What he should have done was encourage Lindsey to go directly to her teammates to see if someone was willing to switch shifts and never gotten in the middle of the decision.

ᐯ   *Leaders choose passive aggression when they feel*
ᐯ   *threatened, insecure, and want to hide from conflict.*
ᐯ   *While the realities of supervising others can be*
ᐯ   *intimidating, even overwhelming—especially for new*
ᐯ   *leaders—hiding behind manipulative behavior to*
ᐯ   *engineer other people's responses is a surefire way to*
ᐯ   *make sure others see you as the worst boss they've*
ᐯ   *ever had.*

Leaders choose passive aggression when they feel threatened, insecure, and want to hide from conflict. While the realities of supervising others can be intimidating, even overwhelming—especially for new leaders—hiding behind manipulative behavior to engineer other people's responses is a surefire way to make sure others see you as the worst boss they've ever had.

How Not to Manage People

- Manipulating employees is fine—it's for their own good.
- Limiting information is a valid management tool.
- It's a valid management technique to pit people against one another; it keeps them on their toes.
- If someone ticks you off, just ignore them. The silent treatment will give them time to work out what they did wrong.
- Praise is like giving treats to a dog; don't hand out too much or they'll come to expect it all the time. Withholding it makes people, like dogs, loyal to you.
- Hand out praise and criticism in quick succession. You don't want your team to get too comfortable.
- Some people say micromanaging is too controlling but, at the end of the day, if you want something done correctly, do it yourself.
- Any success the team has is your success. It's YOUR team, so take the credit.
- Devalue people's contributions by pointing out that they don't have the full picture and let them know, because you're the boss, only you have all the facts.

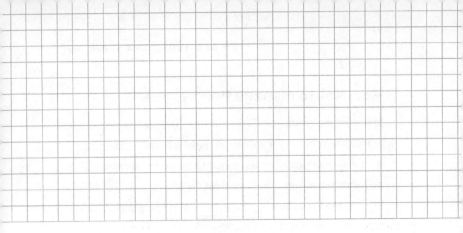

TEN

You're the Boss,
You're Entitled

S ome managers have a skewed understanding of their position. Managers are not the omnipotent Greek Gods of myth moving people around on a giant chess board; they should lead their team, not control or abuse them. Which leads us to a story of a manager who overstepped his boundaries and got a surprise.

HARRIS WAS THE sales and marketing director of a large company selling fitness equipment and his export manager was Jane. It was well known in the office that Harris had a crush on Jane and that he planned to make a move at the biannual sales conference in Las Vegas. There were a number of problems with this, including the fact that Harris was married. Added to that was that Jane not only disliked Harris, he repulsed her. Also, unbeknownst to Harris was the fact that Jane was having a long-term, long-distance, and very secret affair with one of the company's overseas distributors. They had a regular rendezvous at every conference and whenever Jane visited him in England. The company's sales manager, Miles, was close friends with Jane and was the only person who knew the whole story.

At the hotel check-in in Las Vegas, there was a serious problem. Jane discovered that Harris had orchestrated it so that his room was next to Jane's and the room had an adjoining door. This caused problems on a number of fronts, not the least was Jane's plans for a "what happens in Vegas stays in Vegas" few days with her distributor friend.

Miles saved the day by suggesting he and Jane swap rooms. In the very early hours of the next morning, Miles heard the adjoining door softly open, something he had been expecting. He had softened the lighting so he was in semi-darkness and sitting up in bed when Harris walked through the door holding an ice bucket with a bottle of rather good champagne, wearing only a pair of polka-dot, and quite brief, silk boxer shorts. As Harris's eyes adjusted to the darkness, Miles uttered the words that, the next day, when he told the story to his colleagues, made everyone keel over in laughter: "Oh, Harris, I didn't know you cared. Sit down next to me and open that bottle." Harris almost had a heart attack on the spot before pulling himself together and muttering, "Ah, sorry, wrong room."

THIS HAPPENED SOME years ago; today the legal ramifications would have been far worse, as they should have been back then, but

Harris didn't get off scot-free. He managed to make himself the laughingstock of the conference and lost the respect of all those he managed. It wasn't the first time this overprivileged individual acted inappropriately and felt his position entitled him to more than was even remotely reasonable. It wasn't long before he was quietly fired, and Miles took his place as head of the department. If that last story, although true, comes across as a tad extreme, then our next story is all too common. Stephen's story epitomizes how good employees can be abused by poor managers.

STEPHEN, THE ASSISTANT manager at a liquor store, was really looking forward to his weekend. After working overtime every day for the past two weeks, he really needed the time off. And Sarah, the general manager, was finally back from her two-week vacation. Stephen had promised his family that on Sunday (his first day off), he would take them to Lake Okoboji—a two-hour drive from their home in Jefferson, Indiana. On the way they planned to stop at Arnold's Amusement Park.

Early Sunday, he packed the cooler with snacks, loaded the kids and their inflatables into the minivan, and set off on his trip. After an hour riding the roller coaster and taking the kids on a few other rides, they had arrived at the lake and he finally felt relaxed, sitting on an inflatable donut on the water. He decided to snap a few photos on his camera phone of the kids playing in the water. The scenery was so beautiful, and the kids looked so happy. The photos would be prime Instagram material and would show the rest of the world that yes, in fact, he did have a life outside of work.

His fun was short-lived, however, when he received a call from Sarah. Worried that it was urgent, he immediately answered the call. Sarah's voice was demanding. "I need you to come in. Someone called in sick and we don't have break coverage." Stephen explained that he was nowhere near the store, and that he couldn't come in because he was more than two hours away and was with his wife and kids. Unperturbed, Sarah insisted that he drive back immediately and come in to work. She informed him that he was the assistant manager, and it was his responsibility to pick up the pieces. Stephen was that rare breed of dedicated employee that put work above almost anything else, so he begrudgingly packed up and, with crying children and a displeased wife, started driving back to the store. An hour into the journey, Sarah called again to say that everything was fine, someone had volunteered to provide cover, and they didn't need him. At this point poor Stephen didn't know what to do, so to cheer up the children they stopped at a fast-food outlet and were munching their way through burgers and fries when Sarah called again to inform him that she did in fact need him. When Stephen finally arrived at the store, the two employees, whose breaks he was supposed to cover, had already taken their breaks (they took turns eating in the staff room instead of leaving the store) and Sarah was long gone. She refused to stay late (that was Stephen's job) and went to Pilates instead of covering the breaks herself.

IT'S UNDERSTANDABLE IF by now you are shaking your head in disbelief, but that is a true story—only the names and location have been changed. In this case, the general manager felt that she was entitled to leave work when she wanted, and that as her assistant manager, Stephen was required to drop everything and come in to work whenever she called. Ultimately, Sarah expected Stephen to prioritize work above all else.

Stephen's story is not uncommon. According to an article in the *Harvard Business Review*, 94 percent of service professionals claim to work over 50 hours a week, not including the 20 to 25 hours a week that they spend outside of work monitoring their emails.[1] Another article from the same source proclaims, "Better work-life balance starts with managers," and "Companies that educate their leaders on the organizational benefits of providing employees with a healthy work-life balance will see better results [from their employees] than those that focus solely on designing formal policies."

ˇ   *According to an article in the* **Harvard Business Review,**
ˇ   *94 percent of service professionals claim to work*
ˇ   *over 50 hours a week, not including the 20 to 25 hours*
ˇ   *a week that they spend outside of work monitoring*
ˇ   *their emails.*

Being entitled is not always just about making your subordinates do all the work. It can sometimes be about feeling you are above the "law." Neill Marshall of Marshall Koll & Associates, an executive search firm, provides an example of how entitled managers can sometimes feel.

"BACK IN THE 1990s, I worked for an industry-leading recruiting company. We had an office manager who supervised the secretarial staff. At the company Christmas party she got so drunk that she told the CEO to blank off. Her head started bobbing and her head fell forward into a candle lighting her hair on fire. Needless to say, she was fired on Monday."

IN THE END, good managers set good examples, support their employees, and encourage work-life balance, while bad managers (like Sarah) prioritize their own (often selfish) needs above the needs of their employees. Then you have an out-of-control manager who feels she is entitled to drink as much as she likes at an office party, with no concern for the consequences.

How Not to Manage People

- You're the boss; you are like a god to the people who work for you, so acting like one is okay.
- You own these people—you can do whatever the heck you like; they are basically servants.
- Your employees should be 100 percent dedicated to their jobs; work-life balance is for hippies.
- Your expectations should be your employees' reality.

It's All about Communication

othing causes more issues when managing people than poor communication, miscommunication, or no communication.

ELEVEN

Talk More Than You Listen: After All, You Are the Manager

There are managers who talk too much and those who don't talk enough. Both can cause problems with teams and in departments. The biggest problem is with managers who think they are doing a good job but fail to recognize that communication with their team has become one-way. Hjalmar Gislason is the CEO and founder of GRID, a software as a service business in Reykjavik, Iceland. He shared with us how his enthusiasm and desire to share his vision with his team made him talk far too much.

MY TALKING TOO much stemmed from a sincere desire to ensure that my entire team fully understood my vision for the company. I wanted them to feel that I was not only listening to their ideas but giving them due consideration and incorporating them into the company's vision. As a start-up, we held a large number of meetings to discuss the company's mission, goals, and objectives and at every meeting I would go over old ground to ensure everyone fully understood the corporate vision. I'd go out of my way to discover even the slightest difference in their perception as it related to my own. In short, I had a tendency to overcommunicate. I've been guilty of this for my entire career including when I was vice president of a sizeable company in Newton, Massachusetts.

However, it came to a point when I realized this was counterproductive and I decided to figure out at what point in the process I should stop this overcommunication. I soon discovered that the answer was not simple. In my article "Don't Be the Boss Who Talks Too Much"[1] for the *Harvard Business Review*, I came across other HBR articles which commented on complaints from people whose bosses overcommunicated and created a "huge time suck," but then other research from Harvard pointed to "persistent, redundant communication" by managers that actually benefited project management.

This led me to develop and adopt some rules in an attempt to mitigate the negatives of overcommunication (the time suck). At the same time, I wanted to communicate often enough with my team to ensure everyone was on the same page and to overcome any barriers to success. And, I decided, it was vital that all such communication should be two-way.

GISLASON CLEARLY IDENTIFIES the challenges in his article for the *Harvard Business Review*: "When you're trying to communicate your vision and organize the work ahead, it's easy to start speechifying. You have so much to say, so many thoughts on your mind, that you can get carried away. And since you're 'the boss,' other team members may feel a duty to listen and nod along. You can lose track of time."

He suggests that leaders should listen at least as much as they talk, if not more, and in meetings should keep track of how much time they talk as opposed to listen.

ANOTHER TACTIC I use is to engage other team members when I get asked a question, so that they have a chance to add their perspective. My goal is to foster an inclusive environment where people feel their input is valued. I also think it's important to be aware of when people are focused on finding a solution, or actively completing important tasks, and not engage them in unnecessary conversations or meetings. People need unbroken periods of time during which they are free to focus on the job at hand, rather than having to break off to attend meetings.

I think the best times for general conversations are at the start of the day and at the end, with one caveat—don't drag people into a conversation when they are about to leave for the day. I'm also a great believer in one-on-one monthly meetings between team leaders and individual team members, during which they are given permission to raise any issues of concern. To ensure they are completely open I ask them to prepare, in advance, one negative issue or concern to present. I suggest these can be about our products or general concerns about the way we are running the company. They can, of course, raise positive points, but the focus is on addressing problems.

I hold less scheduled meetings than I used to and rely more on ad hoc conversations, which I find more productive. When we do hold meetings, I insist on there being good food available. Low blood sugar is the curse of a good meeting.

If you create an atmosphere of psychological safety and always take into consideration where your team is at any particular time, you have a better chance of communicating with them more frequently, but less annoyingly. Get it right and they'll feel comfortable with letting you know when you are overcommunicating.

GISLASON MAKES A lot of good points and demonstrates the value of being open and honest with oneself when it comes to how we manage people. The first step to becoming manager of the year is to recognize what we are doing wrong. Many managers talk too much under the guise, or belief, that they are being friendly or imparting their worldly wisdom onto lesser mortals, or as in Gislason's case, from a sincere desire to ensure an important message was delivered and understood.

Emily, a nurse in a large city hospital, explained her challenge with her supervisor:

MY BOSS IS wonderful in many ways—she's so nice, she cares about her team, she always has our best interests at heart, but she uses a hundred words when ten would suffice. Sometimes she chats so much I can't get my work done and I feel I'm letting my patients down. Don't get me wrong, some of the time she is offering good advice and information, but at other times she is bragging about her personal life or what one of the doctors said about her. If she wasn't my boss, I'd just excuse myself or walk away, but I'm not sure how to handle the situation. And when I try to turn the conversation back to work and some ideas I have about how we could improve how our station works, she doesn't listen because she's almost always talking about herself.

EMILY'S SITUATION IS as common as litter on the sidewalk and just as frustrating. Managers often become overenamored with their position and their own self-importance, often at the same time as experiencing self-doubt. They become obsessed with their status and try to bolster their credibility with their team members at every opportunity.

Your job as a manager is to lead your team and you can't do that by talking at people; you have to do it by listening and initiating two-way communication, which is the topic of our next chapter.

How Not to Manage People

- You are the manager. Your employee's job is to listen, not interrupt.
- It's important for you as a manager to make sure your team understands what you have to say, even if that means telling them a dozen times.
- It's your team's duty to listen and nod along to everything you say. That is what management is all about.
- If you follow the 80/20 rule, you'll be fine; talk for 80 percent of the time and listen for 20 percent.
- If a team member asks a question, it's your job to answer it; don't solicit input from the rest of the team.

- Meetings are a great way to talk at your employees. Schedule them often and scatter them throughout the day so your team has plenty of breaks from the work they are doing.
- Be friendly, tell employees all about your day, your personal life, and how great you are, especially when they are about to leave for the day.

TWELVE

Talk at People Rather Than to Them; It's Far More Effective

No one ever won an award for being manager of the year by making it all about themselves and talking at people rather than to them. That's not to say that some haven't tried. Tales of managers putting employees on the spot and striking fear into them, and those who fear they might be next, are common. Many of us have been in a hastily convened meeting where our manager starts off asking a few questions and then launches into accusations of wrongdoing. The dialogue is usually one-way and he or she refuses to hear the individual's or team's side of the story.

Trevor was sales manager for a publisher selling, amongst other things, a series of sports books, and while lambasting his sales team at a sales conference, he fell into the trap of ignoring the fact he was talking to real people. This story is told by one of the sales reps, Marcus, who called him out that day.

AT LUNCH, LEE, my sales director, gave me a heads-up that Trevor was going to launch an assault on the sales team over the poor sales of a particular annual sporting almanac. I had already mentioned to him previously that the sales targets Trevor had given the team at the earlier conference were absurd, and he agreed. He knew I was one of the few members of the team willing to stand up to Trevor, so forewarned, I asked for permission to speak once Trevor had finished.

As expected, Trevor launched into an attack like a frenzied pit bull (he too was small and solidly built). Rather than discuss the poor sales of the title in question, he decided to talk at us rather than to us or give us a chance to be involved in any discussion. He harangued the team for the best part of twenty minutes while we just sat there having to take the abuse. I was as angry as I can ever remember being. I just sat there reviewing my notes. He basically blamed us for everything and said he was close to firing a couple of us. The problem was that he was abusing his power and using it to beat us into submission so that his own shortcomings wouldn't come to light. His strategy was to rain down insults on his team and play the blame game, rather than figure out where things went wrong and work with us to understand the situation in which we found ourselves, and perhaps plan a better approach for the following year.

Once he had finished, he was red in the face but looked thoroughly righteous. That's when Lee said, "Marcus, I think you have something to say?" I was in my late twenties at the time and was not known for my patience, or my diplomacy, but in this case I calmly said, "I am appalled at how rudely you have just spoken to your sales force, a team that has been loyal to this company for many years. Also, you have skewed the facts to support your own argument, and even then, many of them were incorrect to begin with." The room fell silent and, if looks could kill, I would not be here to tell this story.

I need to provide a little background at this juncture. The book in question contained sporting statistics and the edition in question was a special commemorative edition, so Trevor was under some pressure to sell more than ever before. The challenge was that it was a specialist publication and almost every sports fanatic already bought it every year—it was far from an impulse purchase. The other major issue the sales force faced was that, as it was a dated title, it was sold on what was then called "sale or return." Trevor had set our targets for this special edition at 50 percent higher than the previous year's edition.

In his dressing down of the team, however, he had quoted sales figures that were incorrect—although, in all honesty, none of us had met our sales targets. His mistake was to use individual net sales figures rather than the actual amount sold by each rep into a bookstore or sports shop. I had accessed the sales figures over lunch and every rep had sold more copies into stores than in previous years—the average increase was around 20 percent.

I stood to make my case, which was that the sales team had sold the maximum the market could handle and more. The proof was in the detailed numbers; in every territory, almost every customer had returned copies at the end of the limited retail sales period (remember, it was an annual publication). The sales force had in fact oversold the book—had they met their targets and forced even higher quantities onto buyers, the returns would have been higher across the country, thereby lowering the profitability of the book. Not only that, customers would have been on the hook for the cost of shipping them back. My coup de grâce was to quietly say that the sales team had not undersold, but Trevor had definitely overpromised the authors and his superiors. The room was quiet, but three directors smiled and nodded at me. I'd made an enemy of Trevor, but it wasn't the first time he had mistreated the people he was supposed to be leading and, within six months, he quietly left the company.

TREVOR DID A number of things wrong, but the biggest thing was talking *at* his team not *to* them, and worse, doing so in a public forum. He could have sat down with them either together or individually and discussed the situation. Unfortunately, he believed from the outset that they were on different sides and he did everything to make that prophecy a reality. When he was originally required to set sales targets for this particular title, he would have been wise to call a couple of his senior reps and ask them what they thought. At that time, the reality of the situation might have become apparent and he could have gone back to his superiors, or the authors, to lower their expectations.

> ⌄ *When in a management role, always be aware*
> ⌄ *that someone, somewhere has access to the truth,*
> ⌄ *and that truth at some point will reveal itself.*

As a leader, he compounded his management mistakes by putting himself in a confrontational situation with his sales team. He was also remiss in ensuring his statistics were correct and his case against his team solid. When in a management role, always be aware that someone, somewhere has access to the truth, and that truth at some point will reveal itself. In this case, Trevor's use of the conference to talk at his team backfired dramatically.

How Not to Manage People

- Never doubt you are worthy of being manager of the year. Impart your wisdom onto the less privileged among your workers.
- Don't bother involving team members or employees in discussions about challenges or problems, just tell them why they are to blame.
- Whenever you have something to say, make the team listen. Just tell it as it is and don't allow interruptions.

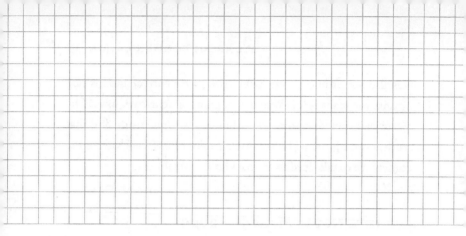

THIRTEEN

Don't Waste Your Time: Only Communicate with People When You Need Something

There are many definitions of the word "communication," but the following one from businessdictionary.com sums it up well from a business perspective: "Two-way process of reaching mutual understanding, in which participants not only exchange (encode-decode) information, news, ideas and feelings but also create and share meaning.[1] In general, communication is a means of connecting people or places. In business, it is a key function of management—an organization cannot operate without communication between levels, departments and employees."

The key phrase in the definition above is that communication should be two-way. Too often, managers fall into the trap of having a symbiotic relationship with employees that is based not on mutualism, but rather parasitism, or at best commensalism.

In the context of the theme of this chapter, mutualism would be communication between the manager and his or her subordinate that would benefit both parties. In parasitism, the manager only communicates when they want something from the subordinate and the interaction harms that person in some way—perhaps by adding stress to their day, giving them added responsibility, or perhaps criticizing them for a mistake or wrongdoing. In short, it benefits only the manager while harming the employee. In commensalism, the manager still only communicates when they need something but the interaction neither benefits nor harms the employee.

The challenge with the three definitions above is that, in reality, any time a manager solely communicates with a subordinate when they want something from that person—even if, on occasion, there is some benefit to the person—they are always harmed over the long term. Employees need the support of their managers; they need to have open lines of communication. Here's a story about someone whose client caused her great frustration and anxiety because of his severe lack of consistency in communication.

MY NAME IS Joanne and I'm a translator. I translate articles, books, reports, just about anything. My largest client is an agency based in San Francisco—they give me a lot of work and everyone I deal with there is friendly and helpful, but the owner drives me crazy by being totally inconsistent in his communication. When he wants something, I get an email marked URGENT—whenever he needs something it is always URGENT and often it's something that is not really my job. Any interaction between us on that particular matter is usually fast and furious. However, when I initiate an email thread, such as asking for feedback on my last translation, or even to question whether it was received, all I get is silence. If, however, a deadline is looming, he'll be all in my face; he'll email me several times to ensure I'm on schedule.

I questioned a particular project contract and emailed the owner. I also cc'd the company's vice president of operations who agreed with me about the issue I had with it and said he'd follow up with the owner. Again, silence for a while followed by several reminder emails from me to both, which resulted in a reply from the owner asking a few questions. *Wow*, I thought, *he's on this* and, within minutes, I provided the answers. That was seven weeks ago and yes, you guessed it, zilch!

Today, I received a series of emails talking about a project's progress, so while I had his attention I emailed back asking for feedback on my list of outstanding issues. We'll see if I get a reply. I doubt it. For the most part this client is the best thing that has happened to my business in a long while, and they have said they love my work, but I am seriously considering looking for a way to be less reliant on them and to wean myself off them. The frustration and anxiety I suffer from working with them is beginning to outweigh the benefits.

JOANNE'S CLIENT PROBABLY has no idea he is causing her so much stress and how close he is to losing a valuable resource (good translators are difficult to find). In some cases, this sporadic communication can be related to a passive-aggressive tendency; in others it is purely a matter of what the person deems as a priority. Busy people believe that their priorities are more important than anyone else's. People with an analytical style, for instance, rarely answer an email or text that doesn't contain a direct question.

> *Review your communication style and question*
> *whether you are focused entirely on your needs or the*
> *needs of the person to whom you are communicating.*
> *If you find it's the former, you may be heading for a*
> *heap of trouble down the line.*

Review your communication style and question whether you are focused entirely on your needs or the needs of the person to whom you are communicating. If you find it's the former, you may be heading for a heap of trouble down the line. And look back at the employees and contractors that you valued but who are no longer working for you: Why did they leave? Check your email archive—was it one-way communication?

How Not to Manage People

- Communication is telling people what to do, how to do it, and when to do it.
- You only really need to communicate with employees, or team members, when you need something from them.
- You're busy. Only answer emails that are urgent (to you) and ignore anything that doesn't have an immediate deadline. If it's urgent, someone will start making enough noise to attract your attention.

FOURTEEN

Keep People on Their Toes, and Always Start with a Negative Viewpoint

For some managers nothing is ever good enough; no matter how hard an employee works, they will always home in on something negative. There is a belief amongst a certain breed of manager that finding flaws in someone's work, rather than focusing on the good work they do, will make them try harder. Nothing could be further from the truth as we see in the following story about a young woman who struggled to do anything right for her manager.

> ∨ *There is a belief amongst a certain breed of manager*
> ∨ *that finding flaws in someone's work, rather than*
> ∨ *focusing on the good work they do, will make them*
> ∨ *try harder. Nothing could be further from the truth.*

CAITLIN WAS PLEASED when she was hired as a junior manager at a retail clothing outlet. From her first day on the job she did everything she could to please Natalie, the store's general manager. Natalie was a textbook Type A personality and a workaholic. Caitlin soon recognized she would have to go the extra mile if she was going to impress Natalie, so she started arriving early for her shift and leaving late. She was quickly meeting her daily goals and cheerfully accepted the increasingly difficult additional responsibilities imposed on her by her manager. Unfortunately, nothing she could do was enough. Natalie never seemed impressed or gave her any encouragement, so over time she became discouraged. One morning, desperate for her boss's approval, she summoned up enough courage to knock on Natalie's office door and ask for feedback on the previous day's close, which had been particularly successful. Natalie, oblivious to the needs of her keen employee, ignored the big picture and focused on minor nitpicking of the previous day's activities rather than the excellent sales revenue. She neither offered solutions, advice, nor future expectations, leaving Caitlin thoroughly disillusioned.

Each day that week Caitlin checked in with Natalie and each day she experienced the same lack of leadership. She received no guidance on how to become a better manager and left the office feeling underappreciated.

The situation came to a head a few weeks later when Caitlin arrived for a solo management shift to find passive-aggressive notes written in capitals on the staff whiteboard. She knew Natalie had left them specifically for her, but of course all the staff saw them too.

"REMEMBER TO EMPTY THE SMALL COMPOST BIN INTO THE LARGER BIN EVERY NIGHT," and "PLEASE LEAVE THE

BATHROOM DOOR OPEN AT NIGHT TO WARM IT UP FOR THE MORNING," and "DO NOT, I REPEAT, DO NOT OVERSTOCK THE SHELVES."

Caitlin assumed that, like in a text message, writing in all caps was the equivalent of shouting. As she stood there, she couldn't decide whether to empty the compost bin on her boss's desk one night and never return, or simply give up and hand in her notice.

NATALIE'S GOAL, IT seems, was to keep Caitlin on her toes. In the end, the next time Caitlin saw Natalie, she was so "on her toes" that she walked straight out the door after quitting on the spot. Natalie was left without a junior manager (and a hardworking one at that); she also had to learn the hard way (after Caitlin wrote a letter to the HR department) about the importance of sandwiching criticism between praise.

> ⌄ *It is such a simple thing to do to focus first on the*
> ⌄ *things your employee or your team are doing well*
> ⌄ *and then provide constructive criticism.*

It is such a simple thing to do to focus first on the things your employee or your team are doing well and then provide constructive criticism. That can be followed by some suggestions as to what to do next, and then maybe, only maybe, and where absolutely necessary—a negative observation.

How Not to Manage People

- Find fault; it'll make employees work harder—it keeps them on their toes.
- Don't give praise, it might go to their head.
- Remind team members loud, clear, and often what their responsibilities are even if there's no evidence, yet, of them screwing up.

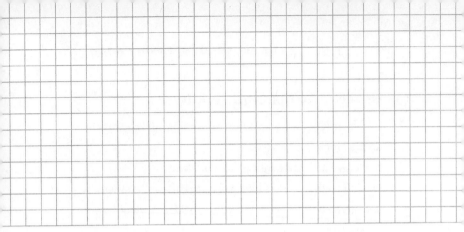

FIFTEEN

Always Make Assumptions—It's Part of Your Job

People jump to wrong conclusions all the time but when a manager does it on a regular basis, it can be a sign of an inability to listen or a belief that they know best. At best, making incorrect assumptions is simply a mistake and, at worst, it's arrogance. In either case it will do little to enhance your relationship with those whom you manage or the clients you service. Often it can happen because your view of the world is different to that of your employee. We all see things a certain way based on our personality style; an analytical person might automatically assume that someone screwed up because incorrect data was input, while a Type A driver personality might jump straight to the conclusion that the person was careless, stupid, or incapable.

∨   *At best, making incorrect assumptions is simply a*
∨   *mistake and, at worst, it's arrogance. In either case it*
∨   *will do little to enhance your relationship with those*
∨   *whom you manage or the clients you service.*

Anne, in our story below, discovers that making assumptions can almost lead you to fire a valuable employee.

ANNE WAS THE CEO of a company that provided on-site leadership training to large businesses and corporations. The company enjoyed an excellent reputation for delivering top-notch, impactful training. Anne was proud of how far the company had come under her leadership and based on her philosophy that customers always come first.

She saw her priority as delivering relevant, meaningful, and long-lasting training for her clients. She excelled in post-event contacts, following up on the impact of the training they delivered and gaining feedback from her participants on how to improve the company's courses. She was a relationship-builder and created a high degree of loyalty with her clients, and as a result, had built the company on repeat business and referrals. Her focus therefore was wholly on the people she was serving—her clients.

Norma worked for Anne as a training administrator. It was her responsibility to ensure that everything ran smoothly with regard to the dozens of training programs being delivered across the country. There are a lot of moving parts when it comes to delivering training in clients' offices, or in nearby hotels, and it was a high-stress job. Norma was well-known for being able to multitask and keep hundreds of balls in the air at any one time. In short, she was a driver personality, a quick learner, a high achiever, and she needed to get things done quickly and efficiently.

Anne, the people-person, and Norma, the backroom wonder, were a match made in heaven—until they weren't. One day, Anne received a phone call from a client who complained about an interaction they'd had with Norma. Apparently, Norma had been waiting for delegate registration information from this client so she could finalize the logistics of the program they were to deliver. With the deadline fast approaching, the client, who Norma had contacted a number of times, had yet to provide the information.

The client claimed Norma had been short with him and that the last time he called she had demanded that he send her the information by the next day. The client told Anne they'd had to make a number of changes with regard to attendees and although, admittedly, he'd been late in providing the info, he felt Norma shouldn't have been rude. Anne apologized and assured the client she would get to the bottom of things.

The next morning, she brought Norma into her office and asked what the situation was with this client. Norma immediately grew agitated. She told Anne she couldn't get her job done properly without the registration information and went into a litany of reasons: there were caterers to organize; decisions about which classroom to book; materials and curriculum to order; and not least, providing the trainer with the final number of delegates so they could finalize their presentations. She explained to Anne that when clients didn't give her what she needed in time, she couldn't guarantee everything would go smoothly, which was unacceptable to her.

Anne told Norma to settle down and remember that the client relationship was the most important thing. Furthermore, she ordered her to apologize to the client and wait for him to provide the information—she was sure she could find a workaround. Furious, Norma stormed out of Anne's office slamming the office door.

Over the ensuing weeks the tension grew between Anne and Norma, highlighting the differences in their personality and work styles. Anne was client-focused and assumed because Norma was process-focused that she didn't care enough about their clients. Almost every time they had to work together, they were snippy, and it often turned into an argument.

Anne was in a tough situation. On the one hand, Norma was an amazing administrator and incredibly good at her job. On the other hand, Anne was having difficulty tolerating what she had assumed was a bad attitude. Norma's dismissal seemed like the only way out of the mess in which she found herself.

Luckily, she shared her work troubles with James, a business friend, over lunch one day. She vented for 15 minutes before finally saying, "The thing is, she is so good at her job! She keeps the wheels on the bus, and everything runs smoothly. Nothing ever falls through the cracks. She's one of the reasons we're so successful."

Her lunch companion asked whether it was truly an attitude problem or more a clash of behavioral style and work priorities. When Anne considered the question, she wasn't sure of the answer. She was in a dilemma; she felt she could perhaps have been more understanding about Norma's situation and perhaps found a way to help, but she also felt strongly that the reason they were so successful was because of the company's client-first philosophy.

James mentioned an upcoming workshop on understanding behavioral styles and suggested that she and Norma might attend together. He said, "Who knows, it might help you see the business from the other person's perspective and prevent you from assuming that your way is the only way."

Anne agreed and registered them both for the full-day workshop. It was enlightening and it became obvious that Anne's nurturing, people-focused, customer-first style clashed violently with Norma's assertive, task-focused, get things done and do them right style. More importantly, they discovered that their differences could be seen as strengths, equally valuable to the company's long-term success. Customers loved being treated well and having all their needs met, but they also valued the clockwork precision of the training session.

The true revelation they had was that the assumption each had about their own importance to the company was just that, an assumption; it wasn't born out by the facts. The reality was that their clients needed what they both brought to the table.

OVER THE FOLLOWING months Anne and Norma significantly reduced the number of times they clashed over anything. They now recognized their style differences during everyday communication and benefited from each other's view of situations. It wasn't too long before the company was back to running like a well-oiled machine.

How Not to Manage People

- You are on the ball. Your first assumptions about a situation will be on point—trust your instincts.
- Don't dig around for the facts; they may contradict what you already know is correct.
- Everyone deals with situations in the same way, so assume they will see the situation from your perspective.

SIXTEEN

If There's a Problem, Focus on Who Screwed Up, Not the Problem

Blaming other people is easy; it's a cop-out for lazy managers. It is, however, common in today's world (perhaps it has always been common); politicians are particularly adept at casting blame. We raise our children not to blame. When Sam says, "Mom, Jenny did it, not me!" we tell him not to be a tattletale. But then in the workplace, as a manager, we often fall into the trap of finding someone to blame rather than addressing the situation.

Vince, the regional manager for a chain of electronics stores, tells the story of one of his managers, Ernst, who managed to make a spate of shoplifting worse by handling the situation poorly. It's a classic case of focusing on the wrong issue and a very common management mistake.

MY MANAGER ERNST had noticed a discrepancy in his store's inventory. Customers would be asking for items that the computer said were in stock but when his staff checked, they were nowhere to be found. At the end of the month, the staff carried out an audit and discovered that the deficiencies were especially high with smaller items such as iPods, headphones, and other peripherals, none of which had anti-theft devices attached. It was obvious they had a serious shoplifting issue. I'd already met with Ernst a few times over the previous months and was on his case about not meeting sales targets, so he was mega-stressed about the fact that profit was literally walking out of the door.

Looking back, I think I should have been a little more hands-on and helped Ernst through a difficult period but at the time I thought he was capable of dealing with the situation. Anyway, he started out okay. He realized he needed a plan of action and that his entire staff needed to be on board. He scheduled a meeting, out of hours, for the store's employees both part- and full-time. He had drawn up new policies and protocols designed to dissuade and prevent shoplifters. The meeting went well and everyone seemed to be onside; he was convinced that they were now fully prepared and motivated to combat the theft issue.

I saw the plan and it seemed well thought out. Employees were to greet every customer who entered the store; the idea was to let potential thieves know their presence had been noted and to keep employees aware of who was in the store at any one time. Second, employees were to closely monitor what Ernst considered the high-risk aisles and also any customer carrying a large purse, bag, or backpack. I remember Ernst assuring me his plan was foolproof. I should have known better.

I visited Ernst at the store the following Monday; he'd been off for the weekend at a wedding and I wanted to check how his "fool-proof" plan had gone. Apparently, he had returned to some disturbing news. The weekend had been busy. On his desk he had found two notes from one of his part-time staff. The first read, "Please check the camera covering aisle six. See 6:45 p.m.: small, old lady with cropped hair. Looked like she put something in her purse, but I wasn't sure." The second noted, "8:10 p.m., tall man in gray hoodie. Think he took something from aisle 8."

After checking the camera footage, we watched the old lady put not one, but three iPods into her small brown tote bag. Neither of us were convinced that she was in fact old. There was something about the way she walked that made us think she might have been wearing a disguise. She was certainly not a kindly grandmother.

By this time, I was not a happy man, but Ernst was positively fuming. We watched as one of the cameras caught one of his cashiers busy dusting and completely oblivious to the grand theft taking place right under her nose. There was more—one of his sales associates seemed to be watching from a distance but never approached the "woman" to check out what she was doing. We discussed why he had hesitated and put it down to either being unsure enough to approach her, scared of the confrontation, or he simply didn't know what the right thing to do was under the circumstances.

Video footage of the second incident did nothing to ease either of our frustrations. As the video started, the camera picked up a man walking into the shot wearing a gray hoodie. He stopped by one of the displays, bent down to apparently scratch his leg, and stuffed a pair of earbuds into his boot. The only sales associate close by was at the end of aisle eight on the wrong side to see the theft. I looked at Ernst and asked him what he was going to do about what we had seen and told him that his plan had been far from foolproof.

I learned what happened next from an employee who was upset by Ernst's handling of the situation. When the two part-time employees who had been lax in their approach to security came in for their next shift, Ernst hauled them into his office and wrote them up for not trying harder to prevent what seemed to be obvious shoplifters. Both were apparently surprised, confused, and upset for what they felt were uncalled-for reprimands.

From my perspective, Ernst should have handled things with a little more care and consideration. Instead of focusing on who may or may not have screwed up, he should have concentrated on the problem. Looking for someone to blame is counterproductive at best, whilst being damaging to staff morale.

If he had taken a more constructive route, he would have identified the fact that the second sales associate was almost certainly unsure as to the correct course of action. He could have then planned some training or coaching as to how to approach and interrogate a suspected shoplifter. I hoped he would have used the camera footage in staff meetings to illustrate that anyone can be a shoplifter, even a little old lady. If he could sprinkle in a few interesting facts, such as one in eleven people in the U.S. are shoplifters, and more than ten million people have been caught shoplifting in the past five years, according to *Loss Prevention Magazine* and The National Association for Shoplifting Prevention, he would have captured their attention and motivated them to take shoplifting seriously.

Instead of playing the blame game as so many managers do, he could have taken some time to study things like possible body "tells" and some of the more common techniques used to spirit goods away in front of video-cams and watchful staff.

Ernst and I had a long chat about how he could be a better manager and, to give him credit, he listened and today he is one of my best store managers.

∨ *Blaming members of your team loses you respect and*
∨ *credibility faster than almost anything else you do,*
∨ *especially if, at the same time, you always take all the*
∨ *credit when things are going well.*

Blaming members of your team loses you respect and credibility faster than almost anything else you do, especially if, at the same time, you always take all the credit when things are going well.

The most constructive thing you can do when an employee screws up is to take a step back from your emotional response and ask yourself, "What is the reality of this situation?" Then accept that reality for what it is and look for solutions rather than assigning blame. Adopt that approach and you are immediately moving forward not back. In which direction do you want your team, your department, your company to move?

How Not to Manage People

- It's always someone's fault; focus on who screwed up and deal with them quickly.
- Always reprimand employees who screw up, it'll make them better next time.
- Focusing on trying to fix the problem is too hard; fire the people who cause it and hire better staff.
- It's not your job to be accountable. Find someone to blame.

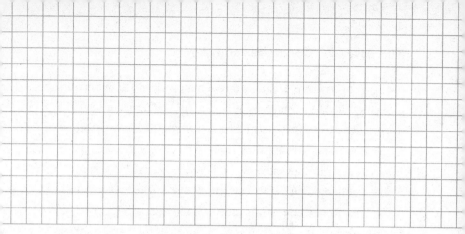

SEVENTEEN

Don't Focus on
How People Feel

In Section 1, we discussed the many ways you can alienate your team. In Section 2, we are focusing on communication and how easy it is to handle things poorly when dealing with the people you manage, especially at times when they are vulnerable.

There's a significant difference between a manager showing sympathy and one demonstrating empathy. Many managers can show, or maybe fake, sympathy but not all have the ability to show empathy. According to a report from Development Dimensions International (DDI) titled "High-Resolution Leadership," only 40 percent of frontline leaders assessed were proficient or strong in empathy. [1] This in itself is concerning, but many studies report that empathy in general is declining throughout society. The importance of being able to feel empathy as a manager is summed up by DDI former senior vice president Richard S. Wellins: "Being able to listen and respond with empathy is overwhelmingly the one interaction skill that outshines all other skills leaders need to be successful."[2]

According to Belinda Parmar, chief geek at The Empathy Business, "The top 10 companies in the Global Empathy Index 2015 increased in value more than twice as much as the bottom 10 and generated 50 percent more earnings (defined by market capitalization)."[3] She went on to say, "In our work with clients, we have found a correlation as high as 80 percent between departments with higher empathy and those with high performers."

Damon, in the story below, has obviously never read anything of the benefits of empathy in the workplace or if he has, he's hiding it well.

RACHEL WORKS FOR Damon in his print shop and three months ago her husband died unexpectedly of a massive heart attack. One day he was playing football, super fit, and the life and soul of any party and then he was . . . gone. Understandably, it hit Rachel hard and she is still grieving—some days it's all she can do not to cry continuously. At the time, Damon had given her five days bereavement leave but it hadn't been enough. She was doing her best to put on a brave face, especially with customers, but she was exhausted all the time and even the most routine tasks, which she had always done without thinking, were now difficult. Deadlines were particularly tough, and she knew her performance was nowhere near up to par.

From Damon's perspective, he was dealing with a liability; Rachel was letting him and the business down far too much. He prided himself on being a hard ass. After all, he had built this business from the ground up and he wasn't going to let one moping employee ruin his reputation or jeopardize his livelihood. For heaven's sake, it had been over three months since her husband died—get over it already.

He called her into his office and told her he was unsatisfied with her work and her attitude and that he was going to have to write her up, and she should see this as her first official warning. If it continued, he would have to let her go. Rachel broke down and shouted, "Can't you see I'm grieving? I'm doing my best. I just need more time."

Damon, who someone had once said had the emotional intelligence of a teakettle, and was certainly as prone to boiling over, was unfazed. He sent Rachel home and told her he expected her to be back and fit for work the following day. Rachel never returned; a friend came to collect her personal belongings and told Rachel's colleagues that the altercation with Damon had pushed her over the edge and she hadn't left her bed for several days. The entire staff felt for Rachel and morale at the print shop was at an all-time low.

DAMON'S LACK OF either sympathy or empathy was astounding, but not all that uncommon. Many owners and managers start from the premise of, "Why should it be my problem?" They turn someone else's hardship into their own, forgetting, or ignoring, that the person they are dealing with is hurting.

> ✓ *Being empathetic doesn't mean being nice,*
> ✓ *although that will certainly help; it means relating*
> ✓ *to the other person, hearing them, seeing things*
> ✓ *from their perspective.*

Being empathetic doesn't mean being nice, although that will certainly help; it means relating to the other person, hearing them, seeing things from their perspective. You don't have to necessarily agree with everything your employee is saying or even agree to what they are requesting. You still have a responsibility to the company and to other employees to make sound decisions, but your employee needs to know that you are truly hearing them, understanding their situation, and empathizing with them.

Damon should have done far more than just monitor Rachel's poor performance; he should have sympathized and empathized with her grief and recognized that her grief was ongoing. Had he for one second thought to himself, "How would I feel if my wife, or my daughter, died—how would I cope with working?" he would have been able to change his perspective. Managers need to focus on how employees feel as well as how they perform because, more often than not, feelings and performance go hand in hand.

Empathy, or the ability to feel it, is vital to successful people management. According to the DDI report mentioned earlier,[4] managers who listen more and have genuine empathy when dealing with staff perform 40 percent better in managing staff overall. They are especially effective in the areas of coaching, planning, organization, and decision-making.

People can't change how they feel, so you as their manager can't use logic, orders, or bullying when dealing with a situation such as the one in the story above. Training yourself to have constructive conversations with employees who are upset, or grieving for instance, is vital to your success as a manager. The key factor in ensuring these interactions are successful lies in your ability to empathize (not just sympathize) with the person to whom you are talking.

Many managers shy away from the "touchy-feely" side of leadership and management, but the ability to feel and show empathy is foundational to good management. As Richard S. Wellins says, "The research shows there is no other single leadership skill that is more important and yet, in today's culture, empathy is near extinction. I believe it is one of the most dangerous global trends of our time."[5]

How Not to Manage People

- Sympathy, empathy—it's all the same; as long as people think you care, that's fine.
- I have empathy. All managers do, but we have a business to run.
- Management has become too touchy-feely; employees don't want you involved in their personal life.
- Being sympathetic or empathetic is a waste of time. It's not as if it'll help improve profitability.
- If someone suffers a bereavement, give them a few days off. After that, insist they get back to work; you have a company to run, it's not your problem.

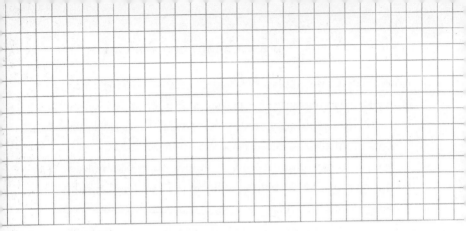

EIGHTEEN

Condescension and Sarcasm Are Great Motivational Tools

The military, at least in movies, has a reputation for breaking people down and then building them back up again. It was, and still is, a training method used by some law enforcement agencies and unfortunately it is common in many workplaces. Some managers feel that they need to strip away all the "bad" habits people might have gained from their previous employment, or have picked up during their career. Others like to break people down as a form of control. A restaurant manager might continually make comments such as, "Is that all you can carry?" or, "No wonder you get less tips than anyone else."

Agustin, who works for a management consulting firm, told us about the following event.

MY MANAGER REGULARLY threatens us as a form of motivation. He really thinks it works to say things like, "Are you trying to get fired?" and "Do you even like working here?" When he became manager of our small division about nine months ago, we were doing really well; we were doing over $1 million in revenues. Today, we're doing about half that. Many of my colleagues decided they agreed with him and didn't like working here and left. I'm currently looking for another job. I'd even take less money to get out of this toxic environment.

SARCASM AND CONDESCENSION are as offensive as they are self-defeating. Both are a form of bullying and lead to lower engagement and increased mental health issues among staff. What is surprising is that it is so common in the workplace and operates in the open. It almost seems to be built into the everyday systems and procedures of many companies. Studies have shown that 61 percent of Americans are aware of abusive conduct in the workplace.[1]

Managers are more often sarcastic and condescending to workers who are performing at a lower standard than their colleagues, or who they don't like as much. And they get away with it because, according to workplacebullying.org, "29 percent of targets remain silent about their experiences."

Often, victims of workplace abuse are seen by managers as being less skilled at their jobs than their counterparts, even when there is evidence to the contrary. Amazingly, some managers reported using put-downs as a motivational tool; they misguidedly believed it was a form of negative reinforcement. Who hasn't heard the classic example of a manager getting very close to an employee and repeating instructions slowly as if the person is an idiot?

Almost one in five people are bullied in the workplace, almost always by someone to whom they answer. The 2017 Workplace Bullying Survey[2] reports that some 60 million Americans are affected by bullying.

Bullying is dangerous to the mental health of employees. More to the point, it's ineffective. Put simply, managers who bully are paying the wages and salaries of employees who have zero investment in their job, or the company for which they work.

How Not to Manage People

- "Break them down and build them back up" is a valid management strategy.
- Employees need to work the way you want them to; how else are they going to learn if you don't put them down and ridicule them?
- Your people need to know who the boss is. Use your power to make it crystal clear.
- Bullying is good for people; it toughens them up.
- Picking on the low-hanging fruit motivates everyone else to do better. Negative reinforcement works.

NINETEEN

Avoid and Exclude Team Members You Don't Like

It's natural in life to like some people better than others; we choose friends with whom we have something in common and hang out with people with whom we feel comfortable. In business, however, it's a mistake to only hire people who we like, or who are mirror images of ourselves. Whether you inherit a team, or you have hired your own team, it's most likely you will have a mix of people working for you; some you like, others not so much. That is the rich tapestry of life; diversity brings great strength to teams and companies alike. Problems arise, however, when we start to show favoritism or sideline team members we don't like.

Michelle is a driven manager; she prides herself in getting work done quickly and efficiently and to do that, she believes she needs to work alongside like-minded people. This story comes from an ex-employee who worked closely with Michelle at an advertising agency.

THE AGENCY WAS busy and was becoming increasingly popular with large, progressive companies. We had just acquired several new clients and we were running interesting and fun campaigns. As we grew, we needed more people and Michelle was given the job of recruiting a number of new team members, which she did with great enthusiasm. It soon became obvious, however, that she was hiring people more on her gut feeling about them than on the skills we needed on the team. Her first four hires were all similar to her in personality, mindset, and had comparable work experience. I even heard her say on one occasion, "The new guys are great, I really feel I can work well with them." She made it clear that she enjoyed the new dynamic they brought to the team.

Things went well for a while but when the next major project came along, she created a new team made up of her recent favorite hires and included a few of the existing team members with whom she felt they would work well. More controversially, and quietly, she assigned all the fun, new projects to them.

This left the "old" team, which consisted of a group of people including myself, with diverse opinions and perspectives, few of which aligned with Michelle's views. She was overheard at one point saying that the old team was dreary and awkward and that they brought down the positive vibe that her new team emanated. This led her to task us with looking after a few older, low-revenue clients, handling rewrites, revisions, administrative work, and stick-handling client problems. Her dream team, of course, continued managing their creative, fun projects for major clients. For the most part, she ignored us and gave us little support. More upsetting was the fact that she would take the "other" team out for after-work drinks and bring cake or other goodies into their private meetings. We all felt ostracized.

Things carried on that way for several months, with a few people on my team leaving to go and work at other agencies. It was then that the wind turned; it became apparent that her wunderkind team approached every project with the same outlook and the same ideas. It was like seven people with only one view. There were no shades of gray; their campaigns were cautious, lacked innovation, and to be frank, were often downright boring. Michelle soon found her dream team's campaigns coming under scrutiny from clients who increasingly demanded changes or rejected them completely. It was obvious to us, although not to Michelle initially, that her team lacked an ability to analyze subjectively what might and might not work for their clients' target markets and product demographics.

It all came to a head when two of Michelle's largest clients decided to take their business to another agency; she had completely lost their confidence through an inability to deliver new, vibrant, exciting campaigns that could deliver customers. It wasn't long before Michelle herself was sidelined by the company. They restructured our division and she became assistant to a well-known manager from another department.

ALTHOUGH MICHELLE WAS good at her job, she was a misguided leader and manager. She honestly felt that by trying to clone herself she would build a better team. Of course, she could be accused of thinking too highly of herself, but that is often true of many people who have risen through the ranks based on their drive, work ethic, and skill. When managers start to believe that there is only one way forward—their way—they begin to lose sight of the benefits of divergent opinions. If you have a team of sled dogs, you need them to all be pulling in the same direction at the same time, but if you have a creative team trying to come up with original, creative ideas, it's no good following the tail of the dog in front. The virgin snow is where you need to go, not the muddied driven ice.

> ✓ *Celebrate diversity, look for outliers to join your*
> ✓ *team regardless of whether they took the same route*
> ✓ *in life or business as you and because they see the*
> ✓ *world differently. Hire someone who is your polar*
> ✓ *opposite, someone who will challenge you at every*
> ✓ *step; it's these people who will stimulate your*
> ✓ *creativity and keep you fresh.*

Celebrate diversity, look for outliers to join your team regardless of whether they took the same route in life or business as you and *because* they see the world differently. Hire someone who is your polar opposite, someone who will challenge you at every step; it's these people who will stimulate your creativity and keep you fresh. Hire people from a wide variety of backgrounds and beliefs—every different opinion is gold because growth comes from unique ideas rather than heading down the trodden path, however comfortable that might feel. Alternatively, fill your team or your company with people just like you and it may feel comfortable for a period, but it will soon become a stagnant pool of exhausted and expired talent.

By excluding those you don't like, or with whom you disagree, you are creating a toxic workplace and that will affect the mental health of all concerned. Team members will leave, and not always the ones you don't like. A negative workplace affects everyone, even those whom you favor. People have a natural need to belong, so it's easy to select favorites and create a clique but people also want to be treated as individuals, not lackeys or acolytes.

Good managers find a way to give every team member a chance to feel included. Poor managers use seemingly insignificant things to ostracize those who are not in their favor. Have you ever greeted everyone with a warm smile, or a handshake, as they entered a meeting but pointedly avoided the person you don't like, or who recently did something wrong? It happens all the time. You may think nothing of it—it's between you and the person you have snubbed, but in reality, you have injected a little poison into the room, into the team, into your company.

It doesn't even have to be as pointed as the example above. Perhaps there is a member of your team who is quiet and reserved; they do a good job but don't say a lot. So, when the rest of the team arrives for a meeting, you laugh and joke with them and, when he or she arrives, all you do is politely nod to acknowledge their presence. In your mind, you have respected the fact that they are reserved, but in fact you have excluded them, made them feel less included. Take a moment to go up to them one-on-one and quietly say, "Thanks for coming, I really appreciate the work you are doing on this project." This will go a long way to make them feel part of the team.

Fostering inclusion rather than exclusion increases productivity. It motivates people, improves morale across a team, and, when done correctly, stimulates creativity and innovation by encouraging a broader cross-section of employees to become involved in putting forth ideas.

How Not to Manage People

- Hire people you like; life's easier that way.
- Building a team with a bunch of diverse personalities is a disaster; people won't agree with you and one another, and nothing will get done.
- Excluding and alienating people is a great way to motivate them.
- Reward those on your team who you relate best to; it will encourage the rest to clean up their act and get in line.
- A good team is one where every member is pulling in the same direction and getting on board with their team members' ideas.
- Hiring people who don't agree with you is a recipe for disaster. No good ever came out of divergent ideas.

TWENTY

Don't Bother Me, I'm Working

M uch has been said about an open-door policy; some business pundits have said that it's a good thing and others have come out against it, highlighting the problems it can cause as a management tool. As with most things, it depends on how you use it in the workplace.

Its most significant downside lies in managers believing that, just because they have initiated an open-door policy, their finger is on the pulse of their business. That is far from the truth. An open-door policy by itself is a passive management tool; people have to come through your door for you to communicate with them and garner information about what's going on in your department, or company. Once there, they usually have a vested interest in what they are telling you, and more importantly, they are only telling you what they want you to hear; you have no idea what they are NOT saying.

One mistake a manager can make when relying heavily on people coming to them for their intel is to believe they have the whole story. For instance, employees may bring you information "behind that open-door" about their coworkers or superiors that is biased; if you then go out and confront someone based on this information, you can put both employees in an extremely difficult position.

On a more positive note, managers who allow staff free access to them do have a better idea of what's happening in their department, which is not a bad thing as long as the information is used with due caution. Allowing casual drop-in conversations encourages the free flow of information, suggestions, feedback, and ideas, all of which makes team members feel valued. The other inherent value is the immediacy of feedback, especially with regard to something urgent. A manager, for instance, who discourages employees from coming and visiting her may have to wait until a planned meeting to discover a project is in danger of going off the rails.

On balance, used effectively, an open-door policy can be beneficial to both management and employees. Of course, some managers still manage to screw it up, like Nancy in the story below.

CHRYSTAL'S BOSS, NANCY, was well-known for two things in the workplace: her insistence during orientation that she had an "open-door policy" and her inability to actually keep the office door open. Chrystal would come in to work every day at the busy recruitment company she worked for and knock on Nancy's office door, at which point she would receive her instructions and tasks for the day. As she left, Nancy always reminded Chrystal to close the door. It was a joke in the office that once Nancy was in her office, she was there for the duration, only coming up for air, for coffee (if it wasn't delivered to her by a member of staff), to use the restroom, or to head home at the end of the day.

Chrystal's story got a little stranger when she told us that Nancy "preferred" for her to call her on the office phone if she had a question rather than walk the few steps to visit her in person. Chrystal reported that it was like visiting someone in a state penitentiary, speaking to someone who was just on the other side of the glass. Nancy never reached out to her team during the day to see how things were progressing; they would only see her if something was amiss and she would need to shout or scream at them. Chrystal often thought that if Nancy's office had a public-address system and a washroom, she would never have to leave her office. Her one-way, open-door policy was resented by the entire team. Chrystal understood that, to Nancy, having the door closed (in her mind, "on occasion") allowed her to focus on her work, but being on the wrong side of the door made it harder for Chrystal and her colleagues to ask questions and establish a collegial working relationship with their manager. They were, effectively, alienated, which made them disillusioned and demotivated.

Chrystal reported that Nancy was clueless as to what went on out in the real office; she had no idea of office politics, interdepartmental challenges, people's birthdays, or anything else. During annual performance reviews, she struggled to remember employees' names and had no idea how those she was supposedly responsible for were managing in their jobs.

Eventually, Chrystal left the company, as did several of her colleagues. She often wonders whether Nancy has even realized she's gone.

NANCY IS LIKE many managers who feel they have an open-door policy but, in reality, don't—they think that by saying it, it makes it real. Some have their door physically open but glare at people who hover on the threshold or tell them they are too busy and to come back later or make an appointment. According to human resources consultant Susan Heathfield, "the purpose [of an open-door policy] is to encourage open communication, feedback, and discussion about any matter of importance to an employee. Employees can take their workplace concerns, questions, or suggestions outside their own chain of command without worrying."[1]

An open-office door is an invitation, not a policy. You need to let your team know how they can interact with you and when. For instance, the open door may not actually be open between certain hours to allow you to answer emails, or deal with administrative matters. Laying down some simple ground rules will make your team feel safe when approaching you in your office. This is important because not everyone is comfortable walking into their manager's office—some relate it to walking into a spider's web. Removing the barriers between employees and management is what an open-door policy tries to achieve; something Nancy did not understand.

Earlier, we read some sage advice from Hjalmar Gislason about the dangers of talking too much and not listening enough. He has a "beyond the open-door" policy whereby he expects his managers to encourage any of their team members to discuss issues large or small. He goes on to say that it's not enough to say you have such a policy, you have to deliver on the promise by demonstrating that when they do open up to you, you take their concerns seriously and take action.

To ensure this happens, he suggests that once a concern is raised by an employee, whether it's one-on-one or at a team meeting, the concern and action taken is tracked, obstacles are identified, and someone is made responsible for its progress. When employees see that action is being taken, they will realize that there is practical value in bringing up concerns and recognize the benefits of open communication.

Whatever open-door policy you adopt, you must realize that it is never enough. Do not rely on it to provide you all the connection you need with your team and your department's projects. Ask yourself, "What am I not hearing? What ideas and feedback am I missing because I'm not listening?" Good managers are good communicators and don't always wait for employees to come to them—they know that only a relatively small percentage will make the journey to their office. Good managers lead the way and connect on a daily basis with team managers; they ensure that over the course of a week they at least make one connection with every single team member.

> ∨ *Good managers are good communicators and don't*
> ∨ *always wait for employees to come to them—they know*
> ∨ *that only a relatively small percentage will make the*
> ∨ *journey to their office. Good managers lead the way*
> ∨ *and connect on a daily basis with team managers; they*
> ∨ *ensure that over the course of a week they at least*
> ∨ *make one connection with every single team member.*

Finally, don't forget any remote workers you might have. They too need to know when it's safe to connect with you via Skype, Zoom, Join.me, or any of the myriad of available video-conferencing interfaces. Figure out a way that they can see your door is "open."

How Not to Manage People

- Having an open-door policy is just something you say; it doesn't mean any dumbass can interrupt you.
- Being interrupted all the time is a nuisance; keep your door closed but hold occasional meetings so the team can have its say.
- My door is never open; there's no need to invite trouble.
- I'm easygoing. No one is nervous about coming to my office to talk to me. Except for Bert—he's just weird.
- It's not as if your office is a confessional. Share what you learn from people in private with the rest of the office, especially if they are complaining about a superior or a coworker.
- Having an open door is more about listening than actually doing anything about what you hear, just sit and nod. It will make the person feel better and then they'll leave you alone.

TWENTY-ONE

You Don't Need to Set and Manage Realistic Expectations

Managers sometimes lose sight of the amount of pressure they put on their employees when they set unrealistic expectations. It's easy to set people to work without setting expectations and just create a list of everything that needs to be done and drop it on someone's desk. Your employee then has a ton of work with no idea of priorities and detailed deliverables. The problem with that approach is that you are, by default, setting expectations in the mind of your employee. You are setting the person adrift without guidance and letting them manage *your* expectations.

Maeve is a writer. She works for an agency writing magazine articles and, because she is good, her manager is ramping up her workload.

I LOVE WRITING and over the last few years have made a bit of a name for myself as both a ghostwriter and author of articles. Unfortunately, my boss, Lila, seems to think I'm superwoman. A few months ago, she decided to have me start work on a book for the magazine. At the time I was flattered and threw myself into writing the book. Since then I've been spending as much time as I can on it, while at the same time keeping up with my regular column for the magazine and writing at least one major feature article a month. I love the fact that I am in demand and that my career is doing so well. The problem is that Lila wants to build my author's platform and sent me a list of ten 1,000-word articles she wants me to write to support a PR campaign to build my profile and, of course, sell more copies of the book. Again, I'm flattered but where do I get the time? She never gives me any guidelines as to what's most important. Is it my column, this month's feature article, the book, or the articles to build my profile?

I feel like she is expecting too much of me and not managing her expectations of me. My own expectations are high and I try to do it all, but in the last week or so I've been snapping at my husband, shouting at the dog, I'm short-tempered with the kids, and I'm tired, oh so tired. Today I sat at my computer and drafted an email to Lila. "Hi, Lila, I quit!" I never sent it, of course. At a time when I should be celebrating my good fortune, poor management is making it feel like a curse rather than a blessing.

WOW, POOR MAEVE has been placed in an untenable situation. On the face of it, her career has hit new heights, but the expectations being subliminally placed on her are unrealistic. A good manager would not continually hand out work without thinking about what that work means in terms of time and effort. Lila should have at least mapped out what Maeve's current workload was and set some expectations that were manageable and on which both she and Maeve could actually deliver. Better still, she could have sat down with Maeve and together worked out what could be achieved over what time frame.

In previous chapters we have talked about managers abusing employees who they think are not performing well, or those whom they don't particularly like. However, there is another form of abuse a manager can fall into and that is burning out a great employee by putting more and more workload on them, setting unrealistic expectations, and then failing to even manage those expectations on an ongoing basis.

> ∨ *However, there is another form of abuse a manager*
> ∨ *can fall into and that is burning out a great employee*
> ∨ *by putting more and more workload on them, setting*
> ∨ *unrealistic expectations, and then failing to even*
> ∨ *manage those expectations on an ongoing basis.*

This chapter could have been called, "It's Okay to Kill the Golden Goose" because that is often what happens. In our story above, Lila may think she is helping Maeve excel and be successful, but Maeve is close to a breaking point and, unbeknownst to Lila, is considering setting out on her own as a freelance writer.

How Not to Manage People

- Don't set expectations—they'll figure it out themselves—or set them ridiculously high.
- If you have a star employee, use the hands-off approach—let them set and manage their own expectations. Focus on the less able employees.
- If you have a good worker, keep piling work on them, they'll be fine with it.

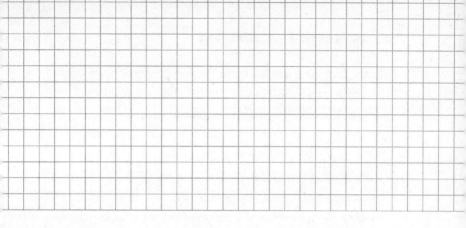

TWENTY-TWO

Make Indecision and Vagueness Your Superpower

Whether you are correct or incorrect in your decision, it's almost always more constructive than being indecisive. Sure, you need time to weigh the pros and cons of any situation but hesitate for too long and situations tend to get more difficult to resolve. Someone once said, "He who hesitates is lost." That is particularly true in the case of managers dealing with human resource issues.

Unfortunately, many managers are like ostriches. They stick their head in the sand and hope the problem will go away; it's like their superpower. However, problems rarely go away on their own; they have a habit of hanging around and escalating and often turn into a gorgon-like Medusa with a head full of living snakes, writhing and spitting venom. The following story comes from an HR consultant who witnessed a personnel issue, which, when not dealt with adequately, had disastrous consequences.

AMY WAS A bright, competent, confident professional in her chosen field of graphic design and communications. Hired by a growing not-for-profit organization as their communications director, she committed herself to her new job as if her life depended on it; and in a way it did—her student debt was outrageous.

Six months later she still loved her job, but was beginning to recognize that there was nowhere to go; she headed up a department of two: her and a part-time assistant. Then the organization's executive director fell ill and was forced to take extended sick leave. Although Amy had not been with the not-for-profit for long, she was the most experienced member of the team and the board asked her to step in as temporary ED until her boss came back. No one had any idea when that might be so she jumped at the chance; it would be good experience and was just what she needed on her resume. She realized it was a rather large jump in responsibility, and she had no management experience to speak of, but she couldn't say no to the opportunity and decided to adopt a "fake-it-until-you-make-it" approach. After all, she thought, it can't be that difficult to manage a small team of four full-timers in addition to her part-time assistant.

Although she knew and liked the five employees for which she was now responsible, she had never really worked with them except when they needed something from her small department. Now that she had to manage them on a day-to-day basis, she suddenly realized she had little idea of how to actually lead a team or manage people.

It wasn't long before she became aware that, although there didn't seem to be any resentment over the fact that she had been made temporary ED, there was tension between two of her new reports. At the first staff meeting Amy convened, Linda and Carly were openly sarcastic and condescending toward each other, and later that month, when they were forced to work together on a small project, you could have cut the air with a knife. Amy dismissed it as small-time office politics—they were not kids and they'd sort their issues out themselves. However, that was not the case and only six weeks after assuming her new role, Amy was sitting across from Linda who was complaining about Carly. She felt Carly disrespected her and was rude and inconsiderate.

Now that a complaint had been made, Amy felt she should do something but had no clear idea as to what course of action to take. Obviously, she knew she should talk to Carly and get her side of the story, but what to say and how to say it was beyond her pay grade, or at least it should have been. She asked Carly to come into her office. Her side of the story was almost identical to Linda's but, in this case, it was Linda who was being disrespectful and rude and a pain in the backside.

Unsure what to do, Amy did nothing. She hoped that by listening to them both, it would give them a chance to cool down and work things out between themselves. She was wrong. The tension between the two women escalated to the point where they were no longer talking to each other, and of course their work suffered. Amy was caught between the two bickering individuals; first listening to Linda's accusations and then Carly's. Still she did nothing

. . . until a major project went sideways, and she was forced to do something.

She called a meeting between the two women and took on the role of mediator. Unfortunately, she had no experience handling such situations and her main goal was not to come across as the "bad guy," so she simply let them reiterate their complaints about each other—more loudly this time—without providing anything by way of guidance. The meeting was not, in effect, mediated, nor did she counsel the two women as to what the consequences of their ongoing hostile behavior and diminished work quality might be if they could not arrive at some sort of common ground and work together amicably. Rather than finding a reasonable and lasting solution, Amy decided to handle the situation by keeping them apart as much as she could and becoming the conduit for any communication between the warring factions.

Although not a completely satisfactory solution, peace reigned for a few weeks until one day, Amy heard Linda and Carly having a heated argument in the kitchen. The argument soon turned into a screaming match and by the time Amy arrived at the scene they were almost at blows. She ordered them to retreat to their offices and cool off. For the rest of the day she thought about what she could do to handle the situation. The following day, a member of the board called to ask what the devil was going on; he'd received a call from a major donor who claimed that Carly had been rude and dismissive to her just an hour previously. Obviously, this was a result of Carly still being angry with Linda and the poor donor getting the brunt of the fallout. Amy's director informed her that this was not the first complaint and he wanted Carly dismissed immediately. Amy knew she had to fire Carly but was indecisive about how to go about dropping the hammer—she had never fired anyone.

In the end, she didn't have to take the plunge—two days later, the board hauled Carly into its monthly board meeting and fired her. Amy was humiliated and lost credibility with the remaining staff for not dealing with the situation early enough, and in the end not having the courage to fire the troublemaker.

Her position had become untenable; she knew her indecision and ineffectiveness in providing clear and direct guidance, and her inability to outline the consequences of their behavior to Linda and Carly, had lost her the confidence of the board. She had lost all authority over her team and felt she had no option but to resign.

THE LAST THING you want to hear a manager say is, "I used to be indecisive, now I'm not so sure." The only thing that gets better with being left to its own devices is a good wine. Challenges in business never get better by being ignored. Good managers make good decisions, mediocre managers make some good and some bad decisions, but at least they take a stand and, if they make a mistake, they can learn from it. Bad managers do nothing until everything comes tumbling down around their ears. Amy went from promising young executive to out on the street, not because she made poor decisions but because she made no decisions.

> ∨ *The only thing that gets better with being left to its*
> ∨ *own devices is a good wine. Challenges in business*
> ∨ *never get better by being ignored.*

Bill Wilson said, "Indecision with the passing of time becomes decision."[1] Therein lies the biggest reason that indecisiveness and vagueness can never be your superpower. It's like Kryptonite—it removes ALL your power; you simply no longer have any control over a situation.

How Not to Manage People

- Ignore a difficult situation; it'll all work out in the end— have faith.
- Don't try to nip work-related issues in the bud; take the long road and see how things develop.
- If you hear a heated argument, close your office door and let them sort it out between themselves.
- Mediation is good for a manager; it puts the onus on solving a problem on the perpetrators, not you.
- Indecision leaves space for things to reach a natural conclusion and that's always good.

TWENTY-THREE

If an Employee Annoys You, Send Them an Email Immediately, Before You Cool Down

There are few people who haven't sent an email written in anger and frustration and regretted it deeply, but some people outdo themselves. Google "email getting on my tits" and you will find many links to an email tweeted by Tom Rabe of the *Sydney Morning Herald* that went viral in 2018.[1] Sent by an unhappy Australian manager to his staff, the email tells his team about "a quick observation that is really getting on my tits." He goes on to berate his team members for playing too much ping-pong during work hours, not dressing in appropriate business attire, for being demanding and exhausting, and for being a cost to the company and to him personally. His coup de grâce was to complain that some of those receiving the email were "taking more sick days than Tom

Hanks during the dying days of *Philadelphia* . . . again with no money on the board." Finally, he threatens to fire several people in less than three months.

The email also made its way into the inboxes of the sender's company's clients and competitors. This led to the manager in question sending out a somewhat half-hearted apology, which said he felt sure the people receiving it "knew" he was only trying to help them reach their full potential.

Randy, a departmental head for an engineering company, sent the following email to his project team of five, after their RFP (request for proposal) didn't win a major contract.

Subject: WE LOST—YOU LOSERS

So, I just heard that we didn't win the contract. What the f**k happened? It was ours to lose you idiots!!!! I told you countless times we needed more case studies and to address their concerns more thoroughly, but you guys were too busy getting off on time every night and spending the weekend with your families. Well, you screwed me, the company, and yourselves because I'm going to fire one or more of your sorry asses unless you find a way to replace the revenue you cost the company. I can't believe some of you even graduated high school let alone have a degree in engineering. You're just a lame excuse for engineers, the whole f***ing bunch of you. If you can't do the job, don't bother turning up on Monday!

Randy

Randy got it wrong on so many counts it's hard to know where to begin. Of course, he should never have sent the email in the first place: It is venomous in the extreme and blames all five people equally with little to no justification. It uses unprofessional and offensive language. It makes threats that he would have difficulty acting on. Losing a contract isn't justification for firing someone, and telling the team they had to replace the revenue or else is laughable. Impugning peoples' schooling and calling them "a lame excuse for engineers" is unforgivable. Sent in a fit of pique, the email destroys the team's morale and loses Randy any credibility with his subordinates. Assuming his superiors get sight of the email, there are likely to be serious career-limiting actions taken against him.

He could have handled the whole situation differently. First he should have accepted the fact they lost and that nothing he was going to do subsequently was going to change that fact. He could have still written the email rant to get it off his chest and then deleted it, before it was seen by anyone. He could then have asked the company that issued the RFP for a one-on-one review of his company's proposal. This would have allowed him to understand exactly why they didn't win and why his competitor's proposal was so strong. He may well have discovered that his knee-jerk reaction regarding a lack of case studies or other information was incorrect and there were other reasons they lost.

Once Randy had the complete story in hand, he could have held a post-mortem with his team to analyze the strengths and weaknesses of their proposal in comparison to that of the winner. In this way, the team would have learned from the experience, rather than being totally demoralized, not to mention offended, by Randy's childish outburst.

In reality, Randy's days were numbered at the firm and, within six months, one of his "losers" was promoted to his position.

How Not to Manage People

- If an employee ticks you off, let them know immediately before your anger wears off.
- If your team messes up, send the whole team an email letting them know they are all fr***ing idiots.
- Ranting emails are perfect for threatening people's jobs. They'll feel your anger and take you seriously.
- What's said in an email stays in an email; it'll never come back to bite you.

TWENTY-FOUR

Share Bad News Via Email;
No Need to Keep It to Yourself

If sending an email when angry can be fraught with danger, so can sending one to announce bad news. Bad news is always best delivered in person, or at least by phone. At times, however, email may be the only way to reach employees, or team members in other locations, or where the sheer numbers make it impossible to let everyone hear the news simultaneously. If, when, and how managers should use email to deliver bad news is the topic of this chapter.

Here's the tale of a manager who had the best of intentions and acted through loyalty to his team but got it oh so wrong. It's the story of an email that came back to bite a guy named Tyler.

TYLER WAS THE general manager of a fast-growing technology company. He was informed by a senior vice president of his parent company that the group had been acquired by a large international conglomerate. Nothing had been formally announced but he was told that there would be significant changes over the next several months that would impact his staff and operations. He was told to sit tight for the time being as more information would be available in a few weeks' time; this was just a courtesy call to let him know that he was safe in his position as GM and he would be responsible for working with the new owners during the transition and reorganization period.

The news threw Tyler into a tailspin. He was somewhat of a catastrophic thinker and was concerned about the impact this turn of events would have on his team. While he had not been given any details, he assumed there was a distinct possibility many would lose their jobs. Depending on who the new owner was, they may well be in favor of global outsourcing. At the very least there would be a lot of retraining and repositioning in their local office. It seemed obvious to him that the business model would change and that their customer base would almost certainly move from a local focus to a global one.

The fact that his twenty-seven staff members had no idea this merger was in the wings lay heavy on him. Many of them had been with the company since its inception, and there had been a significant number of new hires in the last fourteen months to increase capacity to cope with their fast growth. They had built a great organizational culture and the team was close and engaged.

With all this roiling around in Tyler's brain, he came to the conclusion that he ought to warn the team about what was coming so they would not feel blindsided once all the facts were made public. What he was unsure about was how to deliver the message. He felt that sitting with people one-on-one would create anxiety as the information would start to leak out the second the first person left his office, or he put the phone down. And, he couldn't get all his staff in one place at one time. The other issue was that he didn't have answers to the multitude of questions they were bound to ask. In the end, he felt a simple email to everyone was the best course of action.

Hi everyone,

Just wanted to give you a heads-up that our company will be merging with an international corporation. This means there are a lot of changes ahead. Although I have very few details, I wanted to be up front with you all so that you won't be blindsided when the official announcement is made. Let me know if you have any questions.

Tyler

Had Tyler considered this course of action a little more carefully, or perhaps asked his HR department for some advice on how best to proceed, he wouldn't have had to spend the following two weeks trying to deal with people's fears, anxieties, and questions without the benefit of having the answers they were seeking.

The promised few weeks before everything was confirmed and clarified turned out to be several months. Even Tyler's catastrophic thinking couldn't have prepared him for what happened next. Company morale went from highly engaged to super anxious and trust was eroded. A number of quality people quit in anticipation of being let go, and productivity slumped. Absenteeism increased and several people went on stress leave.

Inevitably, when his new bosses came knocking, his once highly successful, profitable company, which had enjoyed an organizational culture that was the envy of the industry, was in shambles.

TYLER IS STILL with the company, but his credibility has taken a huge knock; his new managers never had the opportunity to see his operation in all its glory before he clicked *send* on that fateful email.

Tyler really jumped the gun by alerting people to a situation that was full of uncertainties. Imagine if someone from NASA leaked that a 500-foot-wide meteorite was heading toward Earth and their calculations showed its trajectory coming closer than any other in history and that they couldn't rule out a possible impact. A leak like that would cause unnecessary, widespread panic before NASA could release the full facts, which might be that the timeline was twelve months and that current projections had the meteorite missing the earth by a considerable distance. And, in addition, even if it was coming closer than anticipated, protocols were already in place to prevent impact with the earth, such as using kinetic impactor deflection. This example shows how sharing potentially panic-inducing information widely can backfire.

How Not to Manage People

- Tell your team and employees bad news as soon as you can. It doesn't matter if you don't have all the details; you can fill in the blanks later.
- People handle uncertainty well; they'll be happy to wait patiently until you have further information.
- People deserve to hear any bad news even if you don't have any advice or solutions to offer.

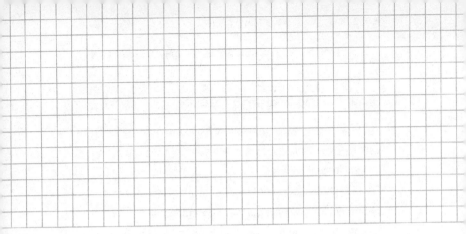

TWENTY-FIVE

How Not to Email

E mail is a wonderful thing, until it isn't. There are so many ways you can mess up with emails, it's surprising that email browsers don't come with warning labels. In previous chapters we've shared one or two horror stories from managers whose management skills left a lot to be desired. In this chapter we have our email blooper reel for you to enjoy. The basic message is, beware the power of email to make you appear like a poor manager.

> ∨ *The basic message is, beware the power of email*
> ∨ *to make you appear like a poor manager.*

JIM SENT AN email to another manager at his firm complaining about how out of shape one of his team members was, or at least he thought he did. He ended his flippant message with, "I'm surprised he can even walk up the stairs he's gotten so fat, and his work has become very sloppy. Maybe time to fire his fat ass." Unfortunately, his fellow manager's name started with the same two letters as his employee's name and he didn't notice that autofill had entered it into the "To:" line, sending it to the poor out of shape man by mistake. Embarrassing to say the least.

⌄ *Double-check to whom you are sending your email.*
⌄ *Furthermore, never commit to writing anything*
⌄ *you wouldn't want to have read in open court.*

TIP: Double-check to whom you are sending your email. Furthermore, never commit to writing anything you wouldn't want to have read in open court.

NATALIE SENT HER team dozens of emails a day, but she was always in a rush and rarely could be bothered to add a clear subject line. One of her favorites was "Subject: Re: Stuff"; another was "Subject: Project." Her team accepted it as another one of her idiosyncrasies, but it became a serious problem when an angry client denied sending her an email six months previously that instructed her to take a specific action, which they were now saying she should not have done. Nicole knew the email existed and that she had forwarded it to her team. However, no one could find the email among several hundred others with similar vague subject lines.

⌄   *Develop a team-wide system for tagging emails so*
⌄   *that when searching for old emails all you need to*
⌄   *do is search for a keyword.*

TIP: Develop a team-wide system for tagging emails so that when searching for old emails all you need to do is search for a keyword.

JOEY WAS ALWAYS in a rush; he was one of those people who prided himself on his ability to multitask, but often it landed him in trouble. He worked for a company selling gas fireplaces and one of his jobs was to send quotes to prospective clients—both retail customers and contractors. One of his colleagues loves to tell the story of when he attached the wrong quotes to two emails—the one meant for a retail inquirer went to a contractor and vice versa. His confusion came about because they both wanted the same fireplace, but the result was that the retail client accepted the contractor price and his company had little choice but to honor the price quoted.

⌄   *Joey's mistake was not a big deal in isolation, but*
⌄   *what if there had been other confidential information*
⌄   *in the email? The message here is that you should*
⌄   *always check that you have attached the file you*
⌄   *have indicated and that it is the correct file.*

TIP: Joey's mistake was not a big deal in isolation, but what if there had been other confidential information in the email? The message here is that you should always check that you have attached the file you have indicated and that it is the correct file.

VANESSA THOUGHT A lot of herself, to the point where she never used a signature line in her email. Even to new or prospective clients, she would sign off with "Best, Vanessa." That came to a sudden stop when her boss marched into her office telling her that he had received an email from a large, new account asking, "Hey, Bill, who the devil is Vanessa?" Her boss also pointed out that, as she seemed to have gotten off on the wrong foot with this new client, he was going to give the account to one of the other managers.

v   *Professional contact information is important, no*
v   *matter how much you may think everyone should know*
v   *your name. You may be the only one who thinks you*
v   *are famous.*

TIP: Professional contact information is important, no matter how much you may think everyone should know your name. You may be the only one who thinks you are famous.

"YO, THIS IS Mikey here. Just touching base, dude." This is from an email received by a director of a firm from a sales manager. Needless to say, Mikey never even got the courtesy of a reply.

v   *Leave informality for emailing your bros, dude;*
v   *it has no place in business.*

TIP: Leave informality for emailing your bros, dude; it has no place in business.

"HEY, TEAM, THANKS for the meeting last week. I'll be sending you the minutes of the meeting once my assistant has time to write them up in between filing her nails." This was received by a junior manager of a law firm, who was a member of the team.

v   *Never try to be humorous in emails. The problem with*
v   *jokes is that someone or something is always the butt*
v   *of the joke, so the possibility of offense is sky high. The*
v   *same goes for religious and political comment.*

TIP: Never try to be humorous in emails. The problem with jokes is that someone or something is always the butt of the joke, so the possibility of offense is sky high. The same goes for religious and political comment.

STEVEN WAS KNOWN for his poor communication skills when answering his team's emails. On one occasion, Stephanie asked, "Which do you want me to do first, the Smith report or the Wilson report?" Steven's answer was, "Yes." He was well known for never answering every question in an email; he'd usually answer the first question but ignore the others. When called out on it, he would apologize and say he was busy and was rushed and got too many emails. This led to his team of seven people deciding to only include one question per email. After a week where he received almost seventy single question emails, he began to get the message.

∨ *Failing to read and answer every question in an email is*
∨ *counterproductive. Instead of dealing with an email*
∨ *once, you will get several follow-up emails in an attempt*
∨ *to extract more information. If you are already busy,*
∨ *would you prefer to deal with one email or six?*

TIP: Failing to read and answer every question in an email is counterproductive. Instead of dealing with an email once, you will get several follow-up emails in an attempt to extract more information. If you are already busy, would you prefer to deal with one email or six?

LIZ WAS ANOTHER manager in a rush; she rarely spellchecked her emails until one day she wrote the following to her small, all-female team and she suddenly realized the importance of checking for typos. "Congratlations on this months' figures. Well done, we trashed the guys in team B! To celbrate, I'd like to invite you all to join me at my dickboxing class after work. Let me know if you can make it."

∨ *Be careful hidden agendas don't come to the surface*
∨ *in your emails! And, especially in business, proofread*
∨ *every message carefully, or you may say something*
∨ *you'll come to regret.*

TIP: Be careful hidden agendas don't come to the surface in your emails! And, especially in business, proofread every message carefully, or you may say something you'll come to regret.

ART IS ALWAYS on his team about professionalism, courtesy, punctuality, and responsiveness, and whenever he sends an email it is always marked URGENT. Unfortunately, Marsha, Jimmy, and Ted, members of his senior management team, report that when it comes to the emails they send him, he only replies on average to one in eight. The others have to be resent multiple times before they appear on Art's radar, or he can't be bothered to answer them. Art constantly complains about the thousands of emails in his inbox, pointing to it as a reason he doesn't always reply. Of course, if we do the math, if his three team members are getting such a poor response rate, they are having to send thirty-six emails each to get replies to the original eight messages. No wonder Art's inbox is swamped.

⌄ *The old time-management tip of only touching every*
⌄ *piece of paper on your desk once holds equally true*
⌄ *for emails. Not answering emails is a downward spiral*
⌄ *to chaos.*

TIP: The old time-management tip of only touching every piece of paper on your desk once holds equally true for emails. Not answering emails is a downward spiral to chaos.

CARMEN WEARS HER heart on her sleeve and it's an emoticon. Carmen, a manager of a not-for-profit organization, has a heart of gold and is one of the nicest people you could wish to meet. Her one downfall is that her emails to employees are overly emotional and personal, to the point that they are not businesslike. She scatters emojis and emoticons like confetti, talks about her family, and brings up personal issues regularly. Not everyone on her team feels this is professional. Sam owns a local business and donates to Carmen's organization regularly. She prides herself on being a consummate professional in business and, although she really likes Carmen when they meet at work-social events, she has difficulty taking her seriously and begins to question how well Carmen is running the office and whether her money is being put to good use.

∨ *There's a time and place for emojis and it's rarely in*
∨ *business. Even if you do have a super-relaxed work*
∨ *environment, you need to choose your audience*
∨ *carefully as, to many people, it can appear*
∨ *unprofessional, especially to customers or clients.*

TIP: There's a time and place for emojis and it's rarely in business. Even if you do have a super-relaxed work environment, you need to choose your audience carefully as, to many people, it can appear unprofessional, especially to customers or clients.

BEN IS A hard-hitting manager; he believes the less words the better and likes it when instructions are crystal clear. All this is good; however, his employees, especially the younger ones, wish that he wouldn't shout at them. Here is a sample of a recent email he sent to employees.

To: All
Subject: UPCOMING ANNUAL SALE!!!!!!

From: Ben Hardwick

I want you all to be on your best game next week for our ANNUAL SALE!!!!! Make sure you wear the AWESOME tee-shirts we had made SPECIALLY for you!

Ben

Unbeknownst to Ben, his employees cringe when they receive one of his emails and mock them regularly. Ben's lack of email etiquette is affecting his credibility with his team.

- ∨ *It's important to keep up with current communication*
- ∨ *trends and protocols, especially if you are an older*
- ∨ *manager and trying to relate to younger people. Of*
- ∨ *course, the reverse is true too; if you are a younger*
- ∨ *manager, ensure your older team members are aware*
- ∨ *of modern terminology and conventions.*

TIP: It's important to keep up with current communication trends and protocols, especially if you are an older manager and trying to relate to younger people. Of course, the reverse is true too; if you are a younger manager, ensure your older team members are aware of modern terminology and conventions.

JEREMY LOVED TO include everyone in emails. His thinking was: the more open any communication is, the better, so he clicked *reply-all* with reckless abandon. His manager, however, had different views, and came to his office to complain about receiving fifty or more emails from him in the previous seven days that had little to nothing to do with her. She said that if that wasn't enough, his habit of clicking *reply all* had landed them in trouble with a contractor. Apparently, Jeremy had created an unwieldly thread between himself, a company client, several team members, and in later emails, a contractor they were employing to work with their client. All would have been well except that the contractor was innocently looking to clarify something within the thread and stumbled upon emails that were only between Jeremy and the client in which they discussed the cost of the project. These "hidden" emails revealed how much the company was charging the client. The contractor realized he was only being offered an amount equivalent to 25 percent of the contract value but being asked to do 85 percent of the work. He had approached Jeremy's boss to renegotiate terms with one heck of an ace up his sleeve! And now, Jeremy's boss was sitting opposite him none too pleased.

ˇ   *Beware of losing control of your email thread so*
ˇ   *that down the line, if someone follows your lead and*
ˇ   *clicks* reply-all, *you don't end up with a breach of*
ˇ   *confidentiality.*

TIP: Use *reply-all* judiciously; not everyone needs to or should be included in all emails even if they are working on the same project. And beware of losing control of your email thread so that down the line, if someone follows your lead and clicks *reply-all*, you don't end up with a breach of confidentiality.

How Not to Manage People

- Never check to ensure you are sending your message to the correct person; autofill is 100 percent trustworthy.
- Subject lines are unimportant; put anything in there.
- If you're emailing someone, they should know who you are and how to contact you just by signing your name. Hey, you're that famous.
- Use "Hey," "Yo," or "Hiya" to introduce yourself. People will think you're cute and accessible.
- Spellcheck will likely catch everything, and besides, a mistake or two will make you seem human and approachable.
- People are cool and will be patient in waiting for your response, especially to time-sensitive tasks and issues. After all, they're all as busy as you.
- Showing emotion in emails, especially using cute emojis, is part of building trust with your team. People will not misinterpret your tone and will be thankful for your candor.
- Use tons of capitals and exclamation marks in your emails. People need to be told what's important.
- Use *reply-all* liberally. People love getting dozens of emails that have nothing to do with them. The intended recipient will appreciate your thoroughness in keeping everyone informed.
- Prattle on endlessly about your personal life. People want to get to know you as a person, so feel free to share everything, in detail: what's going on with your spouse, kids, mother-in-law, dog, new car, etc.

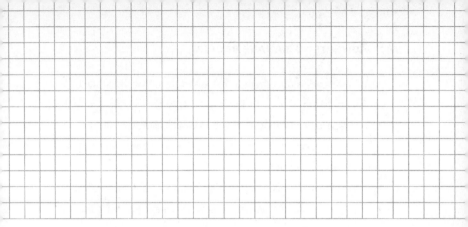

TWENTY-SIX
How Not to Text

Everybody texts these days, it seems. People, especially millennials, prefer to text than email or speak by telephone. Many people even text each other when dining at the same restaurant, at the same table. Without a doubt, it can be an effective way to send quick messages, but it is fraught with danger.

BRENDA HAD A fight with her boss, Daisy, and stormed out of the store. A few minutes later, her smartphone pinged and there was a text from her boss, which read, "Brenda is being the nastiest little bitch today." After realizing she had sent the text to Brenda, not a manager at another store, Daisy ran out of the store to see if she could catch up with Brenda. Unable to find her, she texted her an apology claiming that the text was about a friend of hers with the same name. Brenda reported Daisy to the HR department and disciplinary action was taken.

> ∨   *The problem with texting is that it's so immediate;*
> ∨   *the time lapse between the thought, the message,*
> ∨   *the regret, is mere seconds.*

The problem with texting is that it's so immediate; the time lapse between the thought, the message, the regret, is mere seconds. Here's a story from Brenda, an HR consultant, who fell afoul of the texting gods.

I ONCE TEXTED a client, during a hire I was doing for them, about one of the candidates who had applied for the job. In one of those "not my best moments," I made some unflattering comments about the candidate to my client and sent it. Except it went to the candidate by mistake. The person contacted me and called me out on that unprofessional exchange. I acknowledged my bad judgment and apologized profusely. She could have taken a screen shot of those comments and posted it on social media with potentially serious negative publicity for my business. Fortunately, she took the high road and left it at that, but it could have been much worse.

IF YOU'VE EVER pressed *send* and then realized you've sent it to the wrong person, you will have experienced that sinking feeling because there's no way you can take back either the words or the sentiment.

When texting, never rush; take the time to ensure you are texting the right person. Avoid, whenever possible, making negative or unprofessional comments (even if you are joking or familiar with the person you are texting) that could put you and your business in a negative light should someone decide to make those comments public.

The other major problem is that because we tend to text in a hurry, we rely on autocorrect to do its job properly and that is dangerous territory.

One final story comes from Kimee who works for the owner of a small retail store.

MY BOSS, VIENNA, is really nice, but she is driving me crazy. I think she must be lonely or maybe it's because the only thing she ever thinks about is her store. Whatever the case, shortly after she got a new iPhone she discovered text messaging, and it has become the love of her life. The other day was my day off, and my husband had offered to take our dog out for his morning walk and then bring me breakfast in bed a little later. I was happily dozing, and my phone vibrated; I thought I'd switched it off before I went to bed but must have forgotten. Then it vibrated again, and again, until I finally picked it up. There were five messages from Vienna, two of which had images. "Got in early and tidied the store. What do ya think?" A selfie showed Vienna with her arms outstretched displaying the store, which looked much the same as when I'd left it the day before. The other messages consisted of a list of things she wanted me to do on Monday, and some other inane drivel that

I ignored. Later in the day she sent me a note revealing the day's takings and how she was looking forward to next week when we could dress the store's windows for Halloween. I felt I was being stalked. My husband and I went to dinner and ping! Another damn message from Vienna. This lasted several weeks—the time it took for me to find another job.

IF YOU WANT to text your employees or your team, that's fine, but use messaging wisely and keep it professional. Text only during business hours, and unless people are working over the weekend, never on Saturdays and Sundays. Constant texting is not only annoying for the recipient but also for their spouse or close friends. As a communication tool, it can be both a blessing and a curse. Use it wisely.

How Not to Manage People

- Sending a text to the wrong person is hilarious; even if you say something awful, people will forgive you, it's just a text.
- No one minds the autocorrect bloopers, they're fun.
- Text messaging has made it so much easier to be in constant contact with your employees. Because it's so informal it's okay to text them on their days off and over weekends. It's not like anyone minds a quick text or three.

TWENTY-SEVEN

Don't Take Notes during Meetings; Get Someone Else to Do It for You

Have you ever been to a restaurant with a few friends and the server comes to take the order sans notepad? If he or she then comes back with six correct drinks, appetizers, and entrees, you are duly impressed, right? But what normally happens is they get at least some of the orders incorrect, and you start thinking, "Why the heck didn't the idiot write the order down? Were they trying to be cool, clever, or are they simply lazy?" In any case, their credibility with you drops and so probably will their gratuity.

In business there's another reason why some people, especially managers, don't bother to take notes, and that's because they expect an underling to do it for them. Tabitha, a financial advisor at a financial services company, explains how her manager often plays that card and why it annoys her.

GAVIN'S MY BOSS and he's an okay guy; he knows his stuff and will always help me with a client, or a quote, or any of the legal stuff with which we have to constantly navigate. But during meetings he is so annoying. He has this thing where he arrives at a meeting with nothing: no briefcase, no folders, no notebook, no tablet or computer—you get the idea. You never know whether he's hearing you or not, or whether he's even listening. What really ticks me off is that he picks on me to take notes for him; as if that's my job! Don't get me wrong, I'm happy to take my own notes but if I'm taking his as well, I have to make note of stuff that isn't relevant to me. This means my notes are a mess and what I give him has a bunch of stuff he doesn't need. And don't think he doesn't comment on that!

There's a great story (it was before my time) about Gavin being caught off guard by his boss. Gavin had just returned from an educational event hosted by the Securities and Exchange Commission and was holding the weekly team meeting. Unexpectedly, his boss, Aminah, dropped in on a meeting and suggested that Gavin give the team a CliffsNotes version of what he had learned at the session, especially some new regulations that were going to come into force. Apparently, the look on his face was radical; he started to give a very high-level overview, but Aminah kept asking for specifics. This went on for several minutes before she said, "Gavin, where are your notes?"

His answer brought rolled eyes from his team and he mumbled something about them being in his office. To this, Aminah replied, "Okay, no problem, why don't you pop back to your office and pick them up? I'd really like to hear more of the details, and I think it's important that the team knows what's coming down the pipe from the SEC." Gavin was flummoxed, to say the least, and those that were there that day laugh at how red in the face he became. As one of them said, "If there had been a rock available, he would have scurried underneath it. He looked like he was going to have a heart attack." Gavin managed to extricate himself from the situation by telling his boss that his notes were a mess and it would be better if he presented the overview at the following week's meeting. None of those in attendance knew for sure whether Aminah had seen through his charade but, shortly after, he was passed over for a promotion that everyone thought was his to lose.

YOU'RE A MANAGER; you need to step up and act like one. Managing doesn't mean getting someone else to do everything for you; you've got valuable team members, not servants. In any case, there are lots of reasons why taking your own notes is in your own best interest and will help you become more successful.

- ∨ *Managing doesn't mean getting someone else to do*
- ∨ *everything for you; you've got valuable team members,*
- ∨ *not servants. In any case, there are lots of reasons why*
- ∨ *taking your own notes is in your own best interest and*
- ∨ *will help you become more successful.*

Remember college? You took notes then, or you should have, and that worked, didn't it? Usually the better the note taker, the better the student. The same can be said of managers. Managers who don't take notes often come across, both to their superiors and their employees, as forgetful and unreliable. Think about it: if you have to continually ask team members to remind you about something, how does that look to them? And Gavin is a great example of how you can lose credibility with your boss. Tim Ferriss, author of *The 4-Hour Workweek*, said, "I trust the weakest pen more than the strongest memory."[1]

As we heard from Tabitha, if you arrive at a meeting with no way to take notes, people will think you are not taking the meeting seriously. They will also have difficulty believing you are invested in what's happening, or them, or even actively listening to what's being said. It boils down to respect, and the simple act of not taking notes can be viewed as disrespect. Who knew a pen and paper (or electronic pencil and tablet) could mean so much?

Managers who fail to take notes regularly forget to inform team members of important facts and events. That, in turn, can detrimentally affect productivity. Taking notes allows you to create better reports and collate multisource information. Retaining archived notes can also save you if someone calls into question something that was said at a meeting. In those situations, "Let me refer to my notes" is a powerful statement.

> ⌄ *Note-taking helps you concentrate and focuses your*
> ⌄ *mind on what's important; it's surprising how much*
> ⌄ *more alert people are when they are undertaking an*
> ⌄ *activity during what is primarily a passive process.*

Note-taking helps you concentrate and focuses your mind on what's important; it's surprising how much more alert people are when they are undertaking an activity during what is primarily a passive process. What you choose to make note of is usually more important—it stood out at the time and made an impact on you in that moment. In essence, a significant benefit of note-taking is that it forces you to pay closer attention to the proceedings. Another advantage is that, by taking notes during a meeting, you can jot down questions you might wish to ask when the right opportunity presents itself. Without noting them down, you are likely to forget.

HOPEFULLY, YOU ARE now sold on the value and importance of taking notes. Here are a few tips: It's a good idea to take notes or make an audio recording of all meetings (note: although audio is good, the act of actually handwriting notes has been found to be far more beneficial). If you do decide to make recordings, ensure you get them transcribed; there are a number of online companies providing this service at very reasonable rates.

In the case of one-on-one meetings, it is always advisable to take notes and/or record the meeting. In this way, you will demonstrate you are taking the meeting seriously, and should anything contentious occur, you will benefit immensely from having detailed notes. One more thing: when taking notes, train yourself to write while looking at the person who is talking. Only briefly look down at your notepad or tablet. Tablets today, especially newer iPads, have electronic pencils that allow you to write directly onto the screen. Apps such as Nebo offer you pages on which to write; these allow you to turn handwritten script into type with a tap of a finger. From there it is easy to export to Word and—voila—your handwritten notes become a file ready for your meeting archive folder. Digitizing notes in this way has revolutionized the ease of note-taking.

Make note-taking a habit by finding a way of taking notes that speaks to you; whether that's simply writing everything down in a linear fashion or using mind mapping. How you do it is far less important than realizing the importance of recording information for later use.

How Not to Manage People

- Don't bother taking notes at meetings; make one of your underlings do it for you—he or she has nothing better to do.
- When I don't take notes, people are impressed. They think I have an incredible memory. I think I look cool just sitting there.
- No one says anything important enough for me take notes, and if they do, I can check one of my team's notes later.

It's All about Leadership

Management is more about dealing with the complications of running a division, a department, a company. It's looking after process and its focus is on bringing order, ensuring reliable quality, and profitability—basically steering a safe ship. Leadership, however, is dealing with the constant state of flux we find ourselves in when running a business. Harvard Business School professor John Kotter came up with a wonderful analogy in an article titled, "What Leaders Really Do," which he wrote in 1990: "A peacetime army can usually survive with good administration and management up and down the hierarchy, coupled with good leadership concentrated at the very top. A wartime army, however, needs competent leadership at all levels. No one yet has figured out how to manage people effectively into battle; they must be led."[1]

TWENTY-EIGHT

Don't Lead, Delegate, or Promote Teamwork— It's Not Worth the Risk

M any managers have the title but don't do the job. Sure, they boss people around a little, or a lot, but they don't maximize the value of a team. This chapter takes a look at three areas where managers often fall short.

Teams need a leader, someone they can trust to guide them in managing a project or their workload, someone who has their best interests at heart, and who has and will take ultimate responsibility for the output of the team.

LEILA WAS AN excellent management consultant; she worked for one of the top three accounting firms in its management consulting, risk consulting, cyber security services division. She was a Type A personality and had risen through the ranks quickly. She was a young manager but unfortunately not a good one. The management style she adopted, or rather fell into, was one of telling individual team members what to do and yelling at them when they didn't do exactly what she asked. She treated her team as separate employees rather than as a composite group and often complained to her superiors about the disparate nature of her team.

Becky, the most senior member of Leila's team, continually tried to bring the team together and build cooperation and morale but was hampered by her boss's lack of leadership. Leila had a tendency to always take the credit when something went well and blame the team when anything went awry. At so-called team meetings there would be little discussion about how to proceed with a project. Leila would outline the deliverables and hand out assignments to various people. She rarely took an active role or contributed ideas. When a project hit a rough patch, Leila would tell them that they should KNOW what to do, without being told. She almost never sat down with team members and helped them understand difficult issues and problems and certainly didn't mentor them. The team felt rudderless until Becky stepped up and became the de facto leader, working with the rest of the team to overcome challenges.

This situation went on for a little over a year, until Leila's boss asked Becky to tell him about her role in the team. He had been suspicious of Leila's managerial approach for some time and had been watching how Becky always seemed to be adopting a leadership role on projects. Becky downplayed how much "management" she actually performed and didn't say anything negative about Leila. Two months later, Leila was moved to another division and Becky was asked to take over managing "her" team.

GOOD MANAGEMENT IS not about barking out orders and leaving people to sink or swim; it's not about avoiding responsibility by default. As a manager you are responsible for everything that happens to your team, and for their work. It is up to you to ensure the team has all the support it needs to succeed and, if it fails, you need to own it. That comes with the territory.

MYA WORKED FOR a large and extremely busy superstore in the purchasing department as a junior manager. Her boss, Graham, was an impatient man who found it difficult to teach people, even his managers, to do some of the more complicated and important tasks required in the department. She often thought he had trust issues. From Graham's perspective, if his junior managers started making executive decisions and they messed up, he'd have to redo their work, costing him time and money. His philosophy was, "If you want something done right, do it yourself."

Graham was guilty of both micromanaging and an inability to delegate or empower his staff. Employees had to push and push hard to get Graham to teach them new skills or give them new responsibilities. For the most part, his employees felt they were left in the dark. Compounding this was Graham's eagle eye for detail; he always noticed when something wasn't carried out exactly as he would have done it. His fallback position when anything wasn't completed correctly was to make passive-aggressive comments about his employees' work. He'd grumble and "joke" that it was "hard to get good help these days." This did nothing to improve the team's morale or make individuals feel there was any value in their contribution. Mya wanted to learn new things and take on new responsibilities, but she was afraid of messing up and being on Graham's bad side. So, whenever there was a decision to be made, Mya played it safe and deferred to Graham. Better not to rock the boat, she thought.

One day, however, Mya found herself in a situation where she needed to make an executive decision at work—and she froze. Graham normally put together the weekly purchase orders. If, for whatever reason, he didn't have time to complete them, he would leave Mya a detailed list explaining exactly what he wanted her to order and from which suppliers. On this occasion, however, the situation was different. He had left early that morning for a business trip and she knew he would be unreachable for most of the day. The problem was that he had forgotten to leave her the list, and he hadn't given her the authority to compile and submit her own purchase orders. Mya knew that the orders had to be submitted that day, or else the company would be short on inventory—for a variety of reasons, the deadline was unmovable. She understood how Graham did his purchase orders and the type and quantities he normally ordered, as she had followed his detailed instructions hundreds of times, but she was ultimately afraid to take the risk and submit the orders herself.

When Graham came back to work the following day, however, he realized his mistake. Because no orders had been placed, the company was going to be short on inventory, the shelves would soon be empty, and customers would be angry. When he confronted Mya about the situation, she explained that, in fact, he had never empowered her, or given her authority, to make and submit the purchase orders herself. And that she hadn't wanted to cross a line or overstep and have him angry at her, so she thought it would be best to wait until he was back from his trip and let him make the decision. After all, Graham always made the decisions.

IN THE END, Graham failed to understand the importance of teamwork, empowerment, and risk taking. And Mya was left feeling unsatisfied in her job. Indeed, according to growth strategist Gene Hammett, employee engagement in the United States "is floundering" at about 32 percent. In his *Inc.* article, "Overprotecting Your Team Members Puts Them at Risk. Do this Instead," Hammett writes that "empowerment includes allowing employees to take real risks and fail. Letting employees take over things that contain safety nets gives them some control, but it doesn't empower them to stretch themselves." Preventing employee failure, "out of a reluctance to cede control or a real fear of losing money," ultimately "holds employees back."[1] Rather than criticizing employees who take calculated risks, managers should work to create a culture where risk-taking is encouraged, and employees aren't afraid to fail.

How Not to Manage People

- Don't believe that "teamwork makes the dream work" crap. There might not be an "I" in "team" but there is a "U" in "useless" and "underperform."
- You can do the job better and quicker yourself. Don't waste your time training people.
- Don't let your team take risks. Risks are for companies who want to go bankrupt.
- Make sure your team is afraid to fail. If they fail, scold them quickly and brutally. The more condescending you are, the better.

TWENTY-NINE

Don't Hire Talented People; They May Outshine You!

oor managers hire people that are less talented than themselves in an attempt to inflate their own ego. Think for a second how ridiculous that sounds and how damaging it would be to the growth of a department, a company, and, ultimately, even the manager's career to purposely hire weaker candidates. The reality, however, is that it's not uncommon for managers to act in this way because they have difficulty accepting that people on their team might be better than them at certain skills or in areas of operation. Most of us are competitive by nature and we can fall into the trap of seeing hiring people with superior talent as an attack on our self-worth. It almost seems counterintuitive to surround yourself with people who perhaps can outshine you when interacting with clients and your bosses. Aarav, VP of an international advertising agency, illustrates the difference between two hiring styles and how it can influence a team's effectiveness. He recounts sitting in on two client pitches several years ago at different corporate locations and what he subsequently discovered when he investigated how the two team managers operated.

IT WAS IN the mid-2000s when I decided to carry out a road trip to ten of our offices across the country. One of my goals was to watch our teams make client pitches and write a best practice report to share across the company. I was looking for how well our teams stated the objectives of their campaigns and how well they would deliver on our clients' needs. The bottom line was we needed to show how we could use a client's budget effectively and build value for their brand. While there, I was also interested in team dynamics and how well teams were managed. A secondary objective of my "tour" was to identify candidates for several new senior, head office management positions.

Two pitches stand out from that trip for very different reasons. I won't go into the actual pitch content as that's irrelevant to this story, but will rather talk about management style. The first was a case study in how to woo a client. The manager, Miah, stood up, welcomed the client's team, and briefly outlined the reason for the meeting. She then invited the client to introduce his team members. After this, she asked each member of her team to introduce themselves and outline their individual role and expertise. I have to say, at that point I was impressed. Miah's team was stacked full of talented, experienced, and confident professionals—it was a team of star players. As the pitch progressed, I found myself blown away by the innovation, creativity, and relevance to the client of the pitch. Miah managed with a light hand, only speaking when she needed to keep everyone on track and on point. The smiles on the faces of the client's team members said it all—it was a tour de force and I left feeling sure we would win the account. I also put Miah on my list of managers ripe for promotion.

Two days later in a nearby city, I once again sat in on a client pitch. This one had a very different tenor; when I walked into the conference room, the manager, Otis, was briefing his team and instructing them that he would handle the pitch and only call on them if needed. As I looked around the room, I saw none of the enthusiasm I'd witnessed with Miah's team. When the client's team arrived, Otis welcomed them briefly and immediately went into the company's pitch. He talked for 15-minutes and asked if there were any questions. There were several and he had to defer to members of his team to answer some of the more technical questions. They answered succinctly and well, but with little excitement or apparent authority.

His presentation left me cold. There was nothing new or creative about it—blah came to mind. I could see that the client felt the same and I had little confidence we would win their account. After the client left, I hung around and talked to the four members of Otis's team. What struck me was that they were all low-energy and were lacking in the experience or skills I expected or felt was appropriate. Unlike Miah's team, these people were not stars, they were drones doing Otis's bidding. I couldn't see a spark of originality in any of them. Later in the day, I spoke to Otis's manager about my misgivings and she told me that she was currently reviewing Otis's performance. A year previously, he had taken over a successful team with a closing rate of 81 percent, but three people had been lost to their competitors and, since then, his closing rate had dropped to 47 percent, which, although average for the industry, was far lower than what our company achieved, which was 85 percent.

I took it upon myself to look deeper into the backgrounds of the two teams. What I discovered was that every member of Miah's team was unique; each member brought something different to the table and each had been highly successful and ambitious throughout their careers. There wasn't one of them that wasn't eyeing Miah's job when the time came for her to move up the corporate ladder. Which, I thought, might be sooner than they imagined.

On the other hand, when I took a look at Otis's team, it was a different picture. He had built his team with less experienced, less ambitious people in spite of the fact we paid industry-leading salaries and usually could pick the best available talent. Coupled with the fact that, unlike Miah, he had dominated the pitch meeting almost to the point of excluding his team, I came to the conclusion that he was either consciously or subconsciously hiring people that couldn't outshine him. He obviously doubted his own self-worth. The epilogue to this story is that Miah was promoted and now works with me at our corporate office and Otis works for a small start-up agency, which is struggling to survive.

AARAV'S STORY IS a prime example of the trap some managers fall into when it comes to hiring people, and that is failing to hire the best talent they can afford and attract. Leave your ego at the door when it comes to hiring and surround yourself with employees that can supplement your skills, knowledge, and experience. Never be fearful of hiring people who know more than you do on any given topic; in fact, encourage them to shine. No manager can, or is expected to, do it all. Hiring the right people will free you up to do the things that you are good at, and of course fulfill your duties as a manager. On that point, good managers are also good at hiring the right people; that skill will be seen as a highly valuable one by the people to which you report.

> ∨ *Leave your ego at the door when it comes to hiring and*
> ∨ *surround yourself with employees that can supplement*
> ∨ *your skills, knowledge, and experience. Never be fearful*
> ∨ *of hiring people who know more than you do on any*
> ∨ *given topic; in fact, encourage them to shine.*

Building a highly effective, knowledgeable team is the mark of a great manager and leader. Remember, you are in your management position due to the sum total of your skills, knowledge, experience, leadership qualities, and personality traits. Surrounding yourself with smart people is smart management and a shrewd career strategy. It makes a statement that you are focused on the good of the company and not solely on your own success. And that can be career gold.

As Steve Jobs said, "It doesn't make sense to hire smart people and tell them what to do; we hire smart people so that they can tell us what to do."[1]

How Not to Manage People

- Always hire people less skilled and knowledgeable than yourself; it makes you look better.
- Never hire someone bright enough to someday take your job.
- Ensure you are the most knowledgeable member of your team at all times.
- If you have a rising star on your team, keep them well leashed and under control.
- Don't leave your team members alone for too long—you never know what they might get up to, especially the brighter ones; they need micromanaging to keep them in line.
- Never let your team members present to clients or senior management. The limelight is your domain.
- First rule of management: protect yourself from usurpers.

THIRTY

Always Believe the Worst about People; You'll Usually Be Correct

Some people always see the best in people and give them the benefit of the doubt, and others can't help themselves: they always believe the worst. In your personal life this can sometimes affect friendships or other relationships; in business it can lead to some serious problems, as it did with Clive, the owner of a web development and social media company. In this case we hear from Shelley, an HR consultant who was retained by Clive after he had gone through a particularly costly lawsuit to help ensure his human resource practices were—well, more human in future.

CLIVE HIRED ME to review his HR practices after he got himself into some serious trouble after he fired an employee whom he suspected was not pulling his weight. Clive's was a high-volume business and employees were expected to work long hours to meet client deadlines. Everyone knew this when they were hired. Clive's management style was to allow his staff a lot of autonomy when dealing with their projects; in return he expected a high level of performance and productivity from every designer and technician on his team.

His problems began when a low-profile, rather shy technician became high-profile due to absenteeism. Barry had worked for Clive for two years and had always been a good worker; nothing special but he always delivered, and clients generally liked him. After noticing he had taken a few sick days here and there, he appeared on Clive's radar. Clive started taking more note and saw that Barry was often tired and sluggish at work and his productivity was falling. He was slipping behind with his workload, so Clive hauled him into his office and told him they couldn't afford to take their foot off the gas—clients expected them to deliver well, and on time. By his own admission, Clive was tough on Barry and made it abundantly clear that if he failed to bring his "A" game, he'd be fired. His mistake was in not asking Barry why he was falling behind, or if there were any problems he should know about.

For the next few weeks, Barry arrived at work each day on time; however, his performance was still lackluster and Clive made a point of making eye contact with him and occasionally pointing his finger in his direction while cocking his head as if to say, "I'm watching you."

Clive told me that, by this time, he was convinced that Barry was either partying too much, taking drugs, was just plain lazy, or all of the above, and he'd become dead weight. A week later he fired Barry. What he didn't know, because he had never bothered to ask and had just jumped to his own conclusions, was that Barry was experiencing some serious medical issues that he was trying to cover up for fear of being misjudged—not to mention he was scared of Clive.

Clive discovered this a few weeks later when he received a letter from Barry's lawyer citing wrongful dismissal and asking him to attend a meeting. Clive hired a lawyer and attended the meeting, at which he learned of Barry's illness, which had led to his poor performance at work. Clive's lawyer asked why Barry had not said anything to Clive and was told that Barry had not felt safe enough in his work environment to discuss his condition. Barry said that Clive's bullying and threatening behavior were such that he didn't feel he would be understanding if he had told him why his performance was suffering. Barry's lawyer argued that the company should have taken into consideration his exemplary employment record for two years prior to the situation under review. Threatening to fire him and then acting on it quickly thereafter with no attempt to ascertain the reasons behind Barry's poor performance was de facto wrongful dismissal.

Clive was given the choice of paying a sizable sum to Barry for wrongful dismissal or taking him back in his original position and making accommodations for his medical condition. Making assumptions and jumping to conclusions about employees can be very expensive, as was the case for Clive. Having learned this costly lesson, he hired me to advise him on all human resource issues from that day forth.

HAD CLIVE TAKEN the time to investigate what was going on with Barry instead of making assumptions and jumping to conclusions, he would not have faced some very costly penalties. As we discussed in Chapter Seventeen, there is no separation between work life and an employee's personal situation; the line between the two is so blurred it might as well be nonexistent and, for the most part, it is.

How Not to Manage People

- Rely on your gut; if you think an employee is a flake, then get ready to fire them.
- If an otherwise good employee starts turning up late or missing days, they are probably doing drugs, or they're just plain lazy, so fire them.
- If people can't pull their weight, fire their sorry asses. You don't need to ask why their performance is poor.
- It's a waste of time trying to find out what's wrong with poor performing workers. Best to threaten to fire them— that'll bring them to their senses. Then, fire them.

THIRTY-ONE

There's No Need to Hire People Who Fit Your Organizational Culture

M any managers are fixated on getting the job done expeditiously rather than taking the time to hire, and ultimately lead, the right people to help run their companies. Imani is an HR consultant and has a story about hiring people for the wrong reasons, who inevitably fail to fit into the corporate culture of the company.

"BUT I REALLY like her!" I wish I had a penny for every time a manager said this to me about a potential hire who they thought would be perfect and who turned out to be a disastrous fit for their company. Great resumes do not necessarily equal great hires.

Brinley was promoted to a senior management position at her property management company. It was a great place to work. The business owners really cared about their employees and treated them well. They provided lots of perks and great benefits and gave their employees autonomy and flexibility in completing their job tasks. They had worked tirelessly to create an awesome culture that made people love coming to work. They also expected their team members to uphold the values upon which the company was built, and to contribute positively to the culture they had created. With everyone onboard, there was little drama; everyone got along, worked hard, and felt pride in their individual contribution to the common good.

One of Brinley's first tasks in her new role was to hire an administrative assistant. As this was her first hire, the company provided Brinley with resources including access to an HR consultant (me). However, Brinley decided she knew enough to do it on her own and set about posting the job, reviewing resumes, and scheduling interviews. One applicant, Liz, really stood out to Brinley. She had written an articulate, funny, relatable cover letter, and her resume checked off all the boxes on Brinley's wish list. Brinley reviewed all the resumes and cover letters, but she kept coming back to Liz's, which she read several times. By the time interview day arrived, she was pretty confident who she was going to hire.

Company policy was to interview with a panel, so two other staff members joined Brinley for the interviews. Brinley had purposely scheduled her favorite candidate for the end of the day. While the other candidates interviewed well, and the other managers made notes as to what each brought to the table, Brinley seemed to just go through the motions, waiting for her shining star. When Liz walked into the room, Brinley's eyes lit up. She welcomed

Liz with an enthusiasm that none of the other candidates had received. She opened the interview by asking Liz about something she had seen on her resume, something they had in common—they both loved and worked with horses. For ten minutes, Brinley and Liz connected on their love of horses and Brinley felt like they were old friends.

When the other managers inquired into some of Liz's past jobs, which had only lasted a year or less, Liz was vague and ultimately dodged their questions. When given a scenario question about how she would handle a specific situation, Liz responded with an answer that was quite contrary to the company's cultural values. They also felt Liz's attitude was far too "chummy" and came across as unprofessional.

After Liz left, the managers debriefed the day and put forward their recommendations for who should be offered the job. The other two managers both felt that Celia, who they had interviewed second, had the strongest interview. Not only did she have a strong resume, but they felt she was respectful, professional, and answered their questions directly and honestly. Celia also answered the scenario question with exactly what they would be looking for in a cultural fit.

Brinley was appalled and sang Liz's praises. "I really liked her," she said, "and I think we'd work well together." When the other managers brought forward their concerns, Brinley shrugged it off as Liz being nervous, or that it was something she could certainly work on with Liz. In the end, it was Brinley's decision, and she ignored her colleagues and hired Liz.

Within a month it was clear she had made the wrong decision. While Liz was friendly and well-liked at first, she had a habit of getting too personal with her colleagues and shared far too much about her private life, making her colleagues uncomfortable. Her work ethic left a lot to be desired, and Brinley was finding herself spending far too much time supervising and keeping her on track. Liz's view on teamwork and being a constructive member of a team didn't match the company's, and she was constantly on the wrong side of the company's values. Her lack of buy-in to the company culture was causing problems everywhere and it wasn't long before Brinley noticed people were actively avoiding Liz. During team meetings, there was a palpable tension in the room. Before her three-month probation was over, Brinley had to let her go.

BRINLEY FELL INTO the trap of hiring someone that she liked and with whom she had things in common, rather than bringing onboard a person that would fit with the existing team and who had similar values to the company. According to the U.S. Department of Labor, the cost to a company of a bad hire is at least one-third of that person's salary.[1] As a new senior manager, Brinley was off to a bad start when she allowed her personal feelings to outweigh commonsense hiring practices.

How Not to Manage People

- Only hire people you like. Work's more pleasant that way.
- Only hire people that think exactly like you; that way you'll always agree with their decisions.
- You can hire people that you don't think will fit your organizational culture; they'll be forced to fit in eventually. No harm, no foul.
- If you hire someone and they don't work out, you can always hire someone else. It's not like it costs you much to hire the wrong person.

THIRTY-TWO

Work Is a Place for Work, Not Personal Issues

One of the biggest challenges faced by managers in any industry is dealing with employees' personal issues when they start affecting productivity. Being a good manager is not about ensuring that people do their jobs well at all cost; it's about ensuring that people do their jobs to the best of their ability in an environment in which they feel safe, supported, valued, and heard.

Managers who think that employees should park their personal lives as they enter the building, or even consider this possible, are deluding themselves. Unfortunately, many managers still have this mindset, and often it doesn't end well, as was the case with Norma.

NORMA MANAGED THE customer service department for a large chain of furniture stores. Her team's job was to speak with customers on the phone and deal with product problems, warranty claims, deliveries, and, of course, handle complaints. The work was draining and, on some days, downright miserable. Her hiring philosophy was to choose people who she felt could bring a degree of emotional separation to the job and not be negatively impacted or end up becoming depressed by having to listen to complaints and deal with problems eight hours a day. To Norma, work was work and an employee's private life was just that, private.

Most of the people who worked for her managed to achieve this separation, but a few found it a challenge, especially on bad days when they had to deal with a particularly mean, aggressive, or abusive customer. It was obvious to Norma which members of her staff were coping well and which were struggling, but she felt it wasn't her job to babysit those in the latter category—she had targets to meet and deliverables to exceed if she was going to get her quarterly bonus.

Norma believed, and had made it a goal throughout her management career, that the only way to keep productivity high was to maintain a professional distance from her team. She was once overheard in conversation with a manager from another department saying, "I don't like it when there's too much emotional crossover; before you know it, everyone is up in everyone else's business and talking about their personal lives instead of working."

For the longest time, Norma didn't act on her "no personal stuff at work" belief; people knew to keep it low key. But, as senior management started to put more pressure on her department to deliver more service with less resources, she began to fall back on her skewed management views.

The turning point occurred one day after a week when two of their trucks broke down at the same time and dozens of people didn't get their furniture on the day they were promised. The phones had rung off the hook and it seemed that every person calling into the department was frustrated and angry. Betty, a longtime employee, opened up to Norma that she was feeling the strain; her husband had recently lost his job and she was struggling to keep it together. She also asked Norma whether she knew that teammate Sonya's father was fighting a terminal illness and that was why she wasn't meeting her targets.

What happened next surprised Betty. Norma called everyone together at the end of the day and informed them that their personal lives should not be brought into the workplace or affect their productivity. She left them with the line, "Leave it at the door, folks; your personal shit has no place here and if you can't handle the job because of personal issues you should consider finding employment elsewhere."

Every member of the team was dumbfounded. They'd become close working in a highly volatile and stressful environment. Although they had not spent a lot of time chatting about their private lives, they found support in each other and occasionally met for drinks outside of work.

Norma's unwillingness to be flexible and demonstrate understanding for an individual's challenging circumstances made the workplace feel robotic. Team members felt uncared for and underappreciated. Soon, both Betty and Sonya resigned, and then a month later another person left. The company was situated in a relatively small but prosperous community of 30,000 people with a very low unemployment rate, which meant word got around quickly that the company was uncaring and had unreasonable expectations. As a result, Norma found she couldn't easily replace the people who had left. For Norma, these poor management decisions led to unintended consequences; she found herself immediately short-handed, putting increased pressure on the remaining members of the team, which in turn resulted in an unmanageable workload, and more departures.

It wasn't long before Norma was called into her boss's office to explain why she wasn't meeting her targets and why she was having to interview for several positions to replace people who had inexplicably left—all in the last six weeks. At that moment, Norma got some of her own medicine. She tried to explain what had happened, but her boss said she didn't want to hear all the problems she was having, she just wanted results. After that, every day Norma came to work, the stress grew, her relationship with her spouse became strained, and when she ended up in her doctor's office with stress-related symptoms she finally realized that the separation between one's work and personal life is a very fine line.

ALTHOUGH A TRUE story, it is not often that a manager will be so restrictive on employees' office relationships. The key lesson to learn from Norma is that people are complex beings and can't switch off parts of their personal lives as they enter the work environment. Studies have shown that almost half of employees admit that personal issues have affected their work performance. They can also affect personal well-being, team morale, and inevitably, productivity. As a manager you need to be able to create a balance between caring about your staff and ensuring work gets done and productivity doesn't suffer. In addition, you need to ensure neither you nor your company aggravates any situation an employee may be going through and makes things worse. Remember, you have a large investment in every one of your team and the cost of replacing them and retraining is extremely high, not only in terms of money, but also in your valuable time.

> ⌄ *Being aware of what's happening in your employees'*
> ⌄ *lives, to the degree with which they feel comfortable,*
> ⌄ *is important if you are going to be able to support them*
> ⌄ *in doing their best job. Ignoring an unhappy or troubled*
> ⌄ *worker will result in a drop in both individual and team*
> ⌄ *productivity. On the flip side, you shouldn't try to be*
> ⌄ *their doctor or therapist.*

Being aware of what's happening in your employees' lives, to the degree with which they feel comfortable, is important if you are going to be able to support them in doing their best job. Ignoring an unhappy or troubled worker will result in a drop in both individual and team productivity. On the flip side, you shouldn't try to be their doctor or therapist. Be there for them and do you best to facilitate their passage through a difficult time by reducing work-related stress. Advise them of any resources available to them either through your company medical insurance plan, or perhaps government-related assistance.

If you have an HR department or an Employee Assistance Program, seek their advice. If not, consider hiring an HR consultant to help you work with the employee and figure out what options are open to them and help them find a way forward.

As Ingrid Vaughan of Smart HR says, "In an era where employees have lots of job options, strong managers must see their employees as people, not just workers with a dollar sign. That simply won't fly, especially with the younger workforce. The future of work demands that we put people at the center of every organization by encouraging them to bring their whole selves to work. Inclusive leaders lead from the heart, understanding that people cannot separate themselves into pieces that belong in different slots. Managers who support the whole person when they come to work every day and lead alongside, not above them, will reap the results of a stronger culture, higher retention and productivity, and personal accountability."[1]

How Not to Manage People

- Employees should leave their personal baggage at home where it belongs.
- Keep a professional distance between you and your staff; the minute you get involved in their lives, you're screwed.
- Employees' personal shit shouldn't affect their productivity; at work they should just focus on their job. How hard is that?
- It's not your job to babysit employees when they are going through challenging times in their personal lives.
- Focus on your employees' performance at work and hold them accountable no matter what's happening in their personal lives. After all, what are they going to do, leave?

THIRTY-THREE

Don't Hold Managers Accountable; They Should Know What They Are Doing

Senior management sometimes fails to hold the managers that report to them accountable. In fact, they often have a tendency to disbelieve employees who go over their manager's head and file a complaint. It's seen as somehow underhanded and the word "snitch" is sometimes heard. In other cases, the employee is seen as overreacting, or too emotional. This is especially the case where the manager's department is, on the face of it, doing well. Nothing makes senior management turn a blind eye quicker than positive results, healthy profits, or both.

Here's a story of an out-of-control manager. Nathaniel was a bully. Everyone who worked under him knew this to be a fact. Nathaniel's department was highly successful, and the senior management team knew this to be a fact. They didn't know or ignored the first fact. Several people dropped hints, commented on, and then made informal complaints about Nathaniel's bullying behavior to members of the senior management team. None of them took it too seriously, but when Nathaniel's boss asked him if there was a problem, he answered that it was nothing, just a few people making a fuss about working overtime. He'd deal with it.

Here's the story told by one of the senior management team on the condition that their name be withheld.

NATHANIEL WAS HIRED to manage the marketing department. He interviewed extremely well, had excellent credentials, and we as the senior management team were confident that he was the right person to help take the marketing team to the next level. On the surface, he was perfect. Articulate, bright, driven, competent, he started off with a bang and, within just a few months, our sales increased largely due to his brilliant marketing campaigns. We were thrilled by our hiring decision.

As it turned out, however, Nathaniel was a tyrant. He belittled his team, bullied, and threatened them when they made mistakes or disagreed with him, and held them to an impossible, exacting standard that no one could meet, and then punished them for not living up to those standards.

In time, what had once been a high-performing team began to dissolve into a fearful, stressed group of employees looking for a way out. None of them had felt comfortable going to him directly with their concerns, as no one wanted to face up to his aggressive and bullying style. They knew it would only make them feel worse and wouldn't resolve anything.

We'd heard rumors, of course, but dismissed them as the general moaning and whining you often get from departments that work under a constant high pressure of deadlines and dealing with the media.

That was when two employees came to us with their concerns. It took a lot of courage and we should have acknowledged that, but none of us could imagine it to be true. Nathaniel was personable, and, from our perspective, doing a wonderful job of running the department. I'm afraid we rather dismissed their complaints. Of course, we said we'd investigate but all we did was bring Nathaniel in to discuss the complaints, which he dismissed as a few malcontents stirring up trouble. He assured us everything was under control and the department was still running smoothly, in spite of a few minor HR issues. We believed him and left well enough alone.

Unbeknownst to us at the time, rather than patching things up with the two complainants, he went about making their lives a misery, drawing attention to any mistakes they made, belittling them in front of the team, and making an example out of them at any and every opportunity.

As we had failed the initial two employees, when things got worse, no one else felt confident in coming to us to tell us what was happening. No one wanted to defy Nathaniel.

Soon, the stress level began to show as performance decreased, campaigns failed, and the fractured team crumbled. Sick leave increased, a number of people left, and productivity hit an all-time low. Still, Nathaniel assured us that it was just a series of bad coincidences and he'd have things back on track soon.

Six months after the first two people came to us informally, a longtime employee made a written, formal complaint, which we could not ignore; it had been lodged with the HR department and listed several witnesses. An independent investigation ensued, and more than thirty-five counts of bullying and harassment were identified as being valid. The report, which many of us initially thought was going to be a one-page vindication of Nathaniel, turned out to be sixty-five pages long with over one hundred recommendations from the investigator and cost $20,000. Lawyers became involved, ratcheting up the costs. There was no way to avoid firing Nathaniel, not that we had any desire by that time to protect him. Once the lawyers were finished, there were, of course, many other payments to remediate the suffering Nathaniel had inflicted.

THE DIRECT COSTS incurred due to senior management not listening to and investigating employee concerns, and in not holding Nathaniel accountable earlier, were enormous. The indirect costs were many; there was lost business, lost opportunities, the cost of having employees on stress leave for extended periods, hiring temps, replacing those who chose to leave—the costs kept mounting for several months after Nathaniel left to bully elsewhere.

As mentioned previously, approximately 20 percent of employees are bullied or harassed in the workplace, and 61 percent of them suffer at the hands of their boss.[1] Good management is not just about managing and leading employees; it is also about managing managers.

> ∨   *People find it difficult to confront management*
> ∨   *bullies and just as difficult to report it to senior*
> ∨   *management or their HR department. If an employee*
> ∨   *comes to you with a complaint about bullying or*
> ∨   *harassment, you would do well to listen to them.*

One question you might be asking is, why did it take so long for someone to make a formal complaint to the HR department? The 2017 WBI U.S. Workplace Bullying Survey[2] found that 29 percent of those who are the target of bullying remain silent. People find it difficult to confront management bullies and just as difficult to report it to senior management or their HR department. If an employee comes to you with a complaint about bullying or harassment, you would do well to listen to them; in the long run it will be in your own best interest.

How Not to Manage People

- Most employees are overemotional; if there's a complaint and your manager can explain it, support their story.
- Employees whine a lot—take it with a pinch of salt.
- If you get a complaint about a manager's behavior but his or her department is thriving, you can bet it's a frivolous complaint.
- If your manager says he'll deal with a complaint against him, let him handle it; nothing good will come from you sticking your nose in where it's not wanted.
- Even if a manager is behaving badly toward employees, it's easy to hush it up. It's not as if it will cause any long-term harm to the company.
- Bullying is no big deal, and neither is harassment; all companies experience it from time to time. It'll work itself out in the end. What doesn't kill you makes you stronger.

THIRTY-FOUR

The Workplace Shouldn't Be Fun

Have you ever walked into a business and immediately noticed that it has a great atmosphere? People seem happy, perhaps there is laughter, you are greeted with a smile, there is a background hum of activity, which has a positive, activity-focused vibe to it, and you think to yourself, "I'd like to work here." But then have you also walked into a company where the reverse is true? Silence reigns, you are greeted as if you are a nuisance rather than a potential customer, people are walking by with folders, they have blank looks on their faces, and you think, "Are those people actually automatons?"

JESSICA, A SERVER at a popular burger chain restaurant, loved her coworkers but hated her job. The customers were cheap and demanding, the food that came out of the kitchen was subpar at best, and the management team cared more about keeping labor costs down than ensuring there were enough team members working to keep the shifts running smoothly.

The restaurant would often run out of cutlery because a dishwasher would call in sick, customers would take bites out of their food and find it undercooked, and children would regularly throw ear-splitting tantrums after drinking countless glasses of soda (refills were free, of course).

Despite the many downsides of her job, Jessica looked forward to coming in to work. Her coworkers had become her friends, and they kept her smiling when things got ugly—jokes were a form of currency and traded freely. After all, nobody else understood what it was like to work in that hellhole.

Things changed, however, when Troy, a self-proclaimed micromanager, was hired as Jessica's new shift supervisor. One of the restaurant's core values was that it should be a fun place for people to bring their families. Troy, on the other hand, hated to see any of his staff having fun, which made their already tough work lives intolerable. He would immediately scold any server he found chatting or cracking jokes with another server. His personal mantra, or catchphrase, was, "If you have time to talk, you have time to stock." It was odd, but every time he said this, he seemed to puff up like an oversized tropical bird strutting his stuff.

Troy could not or did not want to see that the servers were already working hard; they wanted to make both their customer and managers happy, but to do this they also had to be happy in their job. His micromanagement style put a stop to all pleasant interactions between servers in the workplace. And by removing those pleasant interactions, Troy took away one of the last things servers enjoyed about their low-paying jobs and therefore they no longer had a reason to stick around.

Within a few months of Troy joining the team, the restaurant's staff turnover rate had doubled. Head office became so concerned that they sent out anonymous surveys to the employees asking them to rate different aspects of their job. Before they left to work at a new and higher-end burger chain across the street, Jessica and a handful of her coworkers filled out the forms. Troy was eventually fired, but not before he had lost the restaurant most of its experienced staff, revenue had dropped significantly, and goodwill was at an all-time low.

IN THE END, making room for fun in the workplace can improve performance levels by keeping employees feeling connected, engaged, and happy. And ultimately, happy employees are less likely to quit their jobs.

- ∨ *Making room for fun in the workplace can improve*
- ∨ *performance levels by keeping employees feeling*
- ∨ *connected, engaged, and happy. And ultimately,*
- ∨ *happy employees are less likely to quit their jobs.*

How Not to Manage People

- Customers don't notice whether your business has a fun atmosphere; they only care about prices and getting what they order at a good price and on time.
- Employees should be glad they have a job. Work isn't supposed to be fun; that's why it's called WORK.
- Fun in the workplace is overrated—when people have fun, productivity suffers.

THIRTY-FIVE

You're the Boss; You Don't Need to Set a Good Example

Here is a story that is a compilation of several stories, which told strangely similar tales. It goes to show how often managers can inadvertently set very bad examples when they let down their guard.

JIM, THE VICE president of sales at a recruiting firm, had just given a presentation to the company's new hires about what it takes to excel in recruiting. He'd talked about high standards, a knack for performance management, and the ability to home in on, and recruit, great leaders.

Feeling pleased with himself, Jim left work early to get ready for the office holiday party, which was to take place later that evening at a downtown hotel. If past experience was anything to go by, some of the junior recruiters would approach him during the night and ask him questions like, "To what do you owe your success?" and, "Why did you choose to go into recruiting?" to which Jim would give his stock replies: "I know talent when I see it," and, "I didn't choose recruiting, recruiting chose me." Yes, Jim was pompous.

He arrived at the party early and, after managing to get through a somewhat awkward conversation with his coworker Gina and her husband, Bill, about the joys of cat ownership, he went to the bar and ordered a rum and eggnog. And another. And another. More people started to arrive, and Jim was already feeling the worse for wear. Like many office parties, the lights were dim, music was playing, and inhibitions were gradually getting lower. And Jim, who was normally reserved, got a little too drunk. The company raffle would be announced soon, and he didn't want to miss it, but he was feeling sick and decided to sneak off to the washroom.

Sometime later he was shaken awake by one of the new recruits who had listened to his lecture earlier in the day. He had fallen asleep on the toilet, pants down, and had at some point slid to the floor. No one knew how many people had seen their vice president of sales passed out drunk on the bathroom floor, but by the number of rumors circulating the company the following Monday, many had witnessed him at what can only be described as a low point in his career.

JIM'S STORY MAY sound extreme; however, it is actually fairly common. Indeed, according to a 2010 poll by human resources firm Adecco, "40 percent of us have suffered a major indiscretion at a work-sponsored holiday event," while, "some 14 percent of us behave so badly that we lose our jobs."[1] In the end, it was Jim's responsibility to set a positive example for his subordinates. His senior position in the company and pre-party presentation about high standards and performance management established Jim as a role model for junior employees. His speech, however, must have seemed highly ironic to the junior recruiter who found Jim on the men's room floor.

Being a good example is not just about keeping your pants up during a work social event; unfortunately, managers set bad examples all the time. Sometimes, people don't even realize the effect their actions have. For example, take the case of a millennial manager who believes strongly in work-life balance and feels it's okay to leave early because the surf is high or a friend is arriving from out of town. His boomer employee may see things very differently; he may view it as another example of his boss shirking his duties. Neither person may be wrong, but the example (good or bad) was set, nevertheless.

Managers who arrive late and leave early, yet expect their employees to be on time, are obviously setting a bad example. Flirting with staff members, showing favoritism, throwing temper tantrums, taking credit for other people's work, being dishonest, telling off-color jokes, avoiding heavy lifting, not having the skills or knowledge required to do your job effectively all set a bad example.

There are hundreds of ways managers can set poor examples, but here are a few that, at first glance, might appear as almost the opposite. Managers who work through their vacation and are always on call, or who are in the office from 5 a.m. until midnight, set a poor example of work-life balance. Employees may see these as "expectations" and try to emulate their boss; this in turn creates stress and even competition between team members, resulting in falling morale and subsequently a drop in productivity, even though, on the face of it, people are working longer hours. Of course, many bosses expound the philosophy of: "Do as I say, not as I do."

∨ *Make no mistake, you are always leading by example,*
∨ *whether you like it or not. You need to be the employee*
∨ *you expect all your staff to be.*

Make no mistake, you are always leading by example, whether you like it or not. You need to be the employee you expect all your staff to be.

How Not to Manage People

- Your employees should do as you say, not as you do, and learn the difference.
- You're the boss; different rules apply to you.
- Getting drunk at a work party is just fine—it's after hours and you're only human.
- Work rules don't apply to out-of-office activities, such as work-social events, or training. It's okay to flirt with that sexy new junior manager.

THIRTY-SIX

I'll Post What the Heck I Damn Well Want

S ocial media is a minefield; ask five people their opinion as to whether bosses should "friend" employees or accept friend requests from them on Facebook, for instance, and you'll probably get five different answers. Then there's Instagram, Twitter, LinkedIn, WhatsApp, WeChat, Snapchat, Pinterest, and dozens more featuring millions of posts daily—any one of which can trip up an unwary manager.

A whole book could be devoted to this topic; however, in this chapter we're not going to do a deep dive into the social mores as they apply to every site, every situation, and every industry. Instead, we are going to provide a brief overview of some of the things that land managers in trouble.

The first thing to realize and accept is that everything you ever say or post on social media has the capacity to come back to haunt you. This chapter could be summed up by saying, "Don't put anything out on social media that you wouldn't be comfortable sharing with your mother, your children, your spouse, your spouse's lawyer, your religious adviser, your banker, the IRS, your employees, your boss, your . . ." well, you get the message.

Rather than give you one story as an example, here are several short examples of how social media can backfire on you in a heartbeat.

> **HUGH WAS THE** executive director of a Christian charitable foundation and, in a momentary lack of judgment, shared on Facebook a joke about a Catholic, a Muslim, and a Jew in a bar. We won't share the joke here, but needless to say, when his board of directors saw it, they were none too pleased.

HUGH NO LONGER works for the foundation, or any not-for-profit organization, for that matter.

> **DAISY WAS A** manager of a recruitment company. While doing a social media dive on a potential job candidate she was considering interviewing, she discovered an Instagram post of the person in the sort of bikini only a Kardashian would wear. She then tweeted a screenshot of it as an example to job hunters of what not to have on their social media pages. The kickback was

substantial, and when the tweet went viral, the company was forced to apologize to the young woman.

IT'S UNCLEAR WHAT happened to Daisy, but she obviously didn't win manager of the year!

CAMERON, THE MANAGER of a web design firm, didn't suffer fools gladly; in reality he felt everyone less intelligent than him was an idiot. And that meant just about everyone. Socially, Cameron was exceptionally popular. He was a charismatic person and, because of his extreme intelligence and knowledge on just about any topic you could imagine, he had a lot of social media followers who believed almost every word he uttered. On one occasion, he posted the following: "New girl in the office today, sweet thing but totally dumb and she's not even blond. It took me an hour to teach her how to answer the phone. What the heck are our schools teaching these kids today? I blame it on the current administration, total a-holes the lot of them. I can't believe HR hired her. I can't believe all the shit I have to deal with every day with all the idiots I have to work with. Rant over."

CAMERON'S POST WAS out of order on so many fronts; it's hard to believe someone so intelligent would consider a post such as this appropriate even to Facebook friends. Of course, it didn't help that several of his employees were also "friends," and it became the talk of the office the next day. In case you didn't catch them all, Cameron's post was inappropriate in the following ways: using "girl" was sexist and patronizing; the reference to "blond" was misogynistic, not to mention generally offensive. Saying she took an hour to learn to answer the phone was insulting and most likely an exaggeration; the political dig was sure to have upset those who supported the administration at the time; and his hit on teachers and the education system was unjustified. And the rant on the HR department was again insulting and wasn't going to win him any friends. Lastly, he alienated all those who worked with and for him. Not bad for only eighty-two words. This shows how dangerous a post can be. We'll never know how much he really meant and how much was said for effect and in an attempt to be clever. What we can say is that he is no longer with the company.

MCKENZIE WAS A party girl by night and marketing executive with a couple of employees answering to her by day. She loved nothing better than to take selfies of herself and her girlfriends partying at clubs both locally and especially during her quarterly, "What Happens in Vegas, Stays in Vegas" long weekends. For the most part, the photographs were innocuous enough; sure, she was always seen drink in hand and obviously a little the worse for wear. Then on one of her trips to Vegas, things got a little out of hand and she woke up just before dawn lying in a corridor of her hotel with her bright red, very short minidress hitched up around her waist. That would have been bad enough, but one of her so-called friends thought it hilarious and posted a picture of her in that position on Facebook and Instagram. The image circulated and took on a life of its own. As she was "friends" with her employees and her boss, her professional image was seriously tarnished and her credibility shot. After being passed over for multiple promotions that she felt should have been hers, she left the company. Although she cleaned up her social media sites as best she could, when she searched for "embarrassing Vegas photos," there she was on several sites. It took her more than a year to get back into a management-level position even close to that which she had lost.

MCKENZIE FELT THAT work and her personal life were separate and that as long as she turned up on time and did her job well, then it was no one's business what she did on her own time. Unfortunately, business doesn't work like that. Managers often have enormous power and responsibility over the people they manage, and the way they handle themselves in their personal lives inevitably has a bearing on their business life. As with McKenzie's indiscretion, remember that it's not just what you personally post that can come back to bite you; it's also what others are able to post or share, especially when you can be tagged.

SALVADOR IS A manager in the financial services industry, and he loves his Shih Tzu called Bella, so he thought it would be a good idea to include her in his LinkedIn profile photograph. The shot of him lying on the floor wearing a Hawaiian shirt with Bella in his arms, also wearing a little Hawaiian shirt and a red bow on her head, was cute, and within days his colleagues were commenting on adorable Bella and laughing. However, it was suggested by a senior manager that a business suit might have been more appropriate—on him not Bella.

ON THE FACE of it, there is nothing too horrendous in the story above, except that it didn't make Salvador look professional, or instill confidence in his ability to handle clients' investments. People love dogs, but your LinkedIn profile photograph should be professional. Preferably, it should be taken by a professional in a studio and not a selfie taken at arm's length.

LET'S RETURN TO the question of whether it's appropriate for you as a manager to accept friend requests from employees. The bottom line is that it's up to you and somewhat determined by the type and size of your company and the industry within which you operate. However, if you want to be completely safe, the answer is to keep business and your private life separate. There are just too many chances that the two worlds will at some point collide and that, when they do, it won't be pretty.

If you decide it's okay to accept friend requests from your employees, is it then appropriate for you to send friend requests to people on your team? The answer to that question is a more straightforward no. The problem is that you are in a position of authority and you can put them in a difficult position. Unless they genuinely want to be your "friend," how do they say no? They can ignore the request, but that is still by default a no, and that might seem awkward and therefore they might feel some pressure to accept. Better to not put them in that position in the first place.

That leads to another issue when the lines between work and home can get blurred. Having insight into your employees' private lives through their online activity can put you in a difficult position when you have to make decisions on things like raises, promotions, and pulling a project team together. You can't unsee what you see online and that bias, or influence, can be a problem.

You may not have considered that knowing about employees' personal issues, such as health status, lifestyle preferences, political activity, and religious affiliations could potentially put you or your company into a difficult legal position. Becoming privy to privileged information comes with a responsibility. Something you say to an employee, or an action you take, could later be tied to the fact that you had access to that knowledge and were therefore biased.

Here's a story that involved a social media post that exposed a manager as an outright liar.

BRUNO WAS COMMERCIAL accounts manager at a company that sold hot tubs. He brought his team together and told them that he would unexpectedly be away for seven days at a conference being hosted by a leading hot tub manufacturer and would be visiting a few manufacturers while in California. He made a big thing about being sorry the timing wasn't better, but that he still expected the multiple major proposals that were due to be delivered to customers to be completed on time. His team buckled down and worked several late nights and were confident they would be able to meet all the deadlines. Then, at a team meeting, one member of the team, Meredith, asked them to gather around her tablet. She showed them a video posted to Bruno's Facebook page by his girlfriend. It showed Bruno participating in a drinking competition aboard a Mexican pirate party ship. The caption read, "Bruno's unstoppable when he's on vacation! LOL." They all looked at the date of the post, which was that day's date.

THE EPILOGUE TO this story was that one of Bruno's team ratted him out to management. He lost all credibility with his team who, from that date forward, believed nothing he said, and when it came to them working late? Forget it! It wasn't long before Bruno was history.

BY NOW YOU can see the dozens of ways in which social media can get you into serious trouble. If you are thinking, "I'd never do dumb s**t like that," there are many other ways you can use social media in a manner that is not appropriate. For instance, there are many stories circulating the internet about managers who pressure employees to promote the company and its products on their personal social media (Facebook and Twitter, especially) sites. Of course, if the employee offers, that may be a different situation. With social media, beware any instance where the line between business and personal becomes blurred.

> ∨   *With social media, beware any instance where the line*
> ∨   *between business and personal becomes blurred.*

In most of the examples above, managers have learned firsthand that personal social media sites can have a negative impact on one's career. These risks, however, can also extend beyond personal social media sites; even professional business sites such as LinkedIn can damage one's reputation. If you're thinking to yourself, "How could LinkedIn possibly have any professional risks associated with it? It's a bloody business site, and I'm not planning on posting any drunken bikini pics or photos of my dog on *that* account," think again. In her *Inc.* magazine article, "Someone Sabotaged My LinkedIn Account," Suzanne Lucas tells the story of a woman whose competitor hacked her LinkedIn account and sent nasty messages to her contacts. According to Lucas, the hacker even deleted the messages so she couldn't figure out which of her "connections" the hacker contacted.[1] Risks aside, however, LinkedIn can be a handy networking tool. As long as you are focusing your posts on business and business education, inviting your employees to be a "connection" may be something well worth pursuing.

Twitter can offer a similar opportunity, but because it is more focused on the opinions of tweeters, one has to be careful when encouraging employees to follow your tweets.

Always remember that almost anything can be found to be offensive by someone. Almost every joke ever told can be considered offensive by someone, even the one about two fish swimming along and when they hit a wall, one says to the other, "Dam." The fact that this is a double entendre on the word "damn" could still offend someone. Seriously. Thinking back to the story set in Vegas earlier, I suppose one could say, "Anything that appears on social media stays on social media—forever!"

How Not to Manage People

- Don't worry, anything you post on Facebook will only ever be seen by your close friends.
- "Friending" all your employees on Facebook and other media sites shows you are cool and open. No harm in that!
- "Friend" everyone on your team and put pressure on them to accept—it builds team spirit. Plus you can then see what they do in their personal life. It's a win-win.
- No one is going to be offended by that joke you posted about a local or national politician, ethnic or religious

group, or if you poke fun at the new hire at work or whatever—it's all in good fun. Social media has a short afterlife.

- Your personal life is just that, personal. If you want to post photographs of you partying in Vegas on Instagram that's your right. It has nothing to do with your boss or your subordinates.

- Have fun with your LinkedIn profile; that photograph of you with your family and Sonny your golden retriever is fine; it makes you look approachable.

- Social media only works one way; you can post whatever you like. Your employees can't do anything about it.

- Business social media sites such as LinkedIn are 100 percent safe; no one could possibly hack your account and pretend they are you to your connections.

THIRTY-SEVEN

Tomorrow's Manager of the Year

Hopefully this book will have given you an idea of what not to do if you hope to win manager of the year, or at least be in the running. The basics of good management and leadership haven't changed a lot over the years, but the emphasis has. For instance, in the past, management was hierarchical with instructions coming down from on high and filtering down to the people and teams that actually did the work. Today, organizations are flatter and there is less middle management to contend with; managers are closer to the action than ever before.

The other change is that today we live in a multigenerational work environment, with each generation having a unique view on how their workplace should look. We have boomers managing millennials and Gen Xers and vice versa; this is a result of increasing numbers of boomers hanging around in the workplace far longer than expected. We've already discussed some of the differences in work-life balance these generations exhibit. But it is worth mentioning here that, to be successful, today's manager should grasp the opportunity to learn from this intergenerational wealth of knowledge, experience, and yes, perspective on work itself.

In the coming years, management will be a far more collaborative affair. Engagement will be a vital component of success when building teams or companies. Open thinking, feedback, innovation, and creative thinking will be critical. Tomorrow's managers will need to be more open than ever before to input from their teams and their employees, and they will need to consistently bring onboard creative thinkers. Empowerment and trust will become increasingly important. In short, the best managers will be those who build the most cohesive teams.

> ∨ *Tomorrow's managers will need to be more open*
> ∨ *than ever before to input from their teams and their*
> ∨ *employees, and they will need to consistently bring*
> ∨ *onboard creative thinkers. Empowerment and trust*
> ∨ *will become increasingly important. In short, the best*
> ∨ *managers will be those who build the most cohesive*
> ∨ *teams.*

The business environment has never been as fast-moving as it is today, and new technology will require out-of-the-box thinking by managers and their teams. The average twenty-year-old today will likely have five careers during his or her lifetime, and managers will face constant change within the teams they manage. To cope with this, and to minimize turnover, mentoring and coaching will play a prominent part in team management and team culture.

Organizational culture, which has always been important, will become increasingly so, and managers will need to cultivate and protect their company's beliefs and values by hiring people that naturally fit their corporate philosophy. Given the multigenerational business world we live in, this might present a challenge. For instance, today's millennial managers are less concerned with how the game is played—that is, they care less how results are achieved, as long as they are achieved. Number of hours or weekends worked, type of clothing worn to the office, and the work environment are far less relevant than the output achieved. This is a reality to which some baby boomers might not easily adapt.

Although AI is already making a high percentage of hiring decisions at major corporations such as IBM (AI has replaced almost one-third of IBM's HR staff), people skills in management roles remain a vital component of good management.[1]

What hasn't changed is that if you want to win that manager of the year award, you need to exhibit strong leadership traits, such as integrity, honesty, fairness, and transparency. That is how you will build winning teams. You need to be open, communicative, inclusive, and charismatic. You need to park your ego, be a guide, don't micromanage, empower your people by trusting them, value their input, and focus on the team and each business goal, not your own personal agenda. Team success is the only way you will ever win "manager of the year." Of course, if you do it right, you'll prefer to win "team of the year."

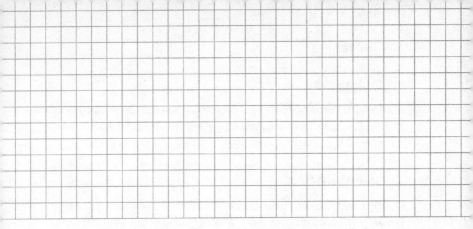

Notes

Introduction

1. Mental Health America, "2019 Mind the Workplace Report," https://www.mhanational.org/get-involved/download-2019-mind-workplace-report.

Chapter 6

1. Gloria Steinem, www.gloriasteinem.com.

Chapter 9

1. Mental Health America, "2019 Mind the Workplace Report."

2. Eric C. Hansen and Ron A. Carucci, *Rising to Power*.

Chapter 10

1. Leslie A. Perlow and Jessica L. Porter, "Making Time Off Predictable—and Required," *Harvard Business Review*, October 2009, https://hbr.org/2009/10/making-time-off-predictable-and-required.

Chapter 11

1. Hjalmar Gislason, "Don't Be the Boss Who Talks Too Much," *Harvard Business Review*, May 3, 2019, https://hbr.org/2019/05/dont-be-the-boss-who-talks-too-much.

Chapter 13

1. Business Dictionary Definition, http://www.businessdictionary.com/definition/communication.html.

Chapter 17

1. "High-Resolution Leadership," DDI (Development Dimensions International), https://www.ddiworld.com/hirezleadership.

2. "What's the Number 1 Leadership Skill for Overall Success?" DDI, February 23, 2016, https://www.ddiworld.com/global-offices/united-states/press-room/what-is-the-1-leadership-skill-for-overall-success.

3. Belinda Parmar, "The Most Empathetic Companies, 2016," *Harvard Business Review*, December 20, 2016, https://hbr.org/2016/12/the-most-and-least-empathetic-companies-2016.

4. "High-Resolution Leadership," DDI.

5. "What's the Number 1 Leadership Skill for Overall Success?" DDI.

Chapter 18

1. "A Modern Tale of Witnesses Doing Nothing, Except When . . ." Workplace Bullying Institute, October 27, 2017, https://www.workplacebullying.org/category/science/.

2. Gary Namie, PhD, "Results In: 2017 WBI U.S. Workplace Bullying Survey," Workplace Bullying Institute, June 13, 2017, https://www.workplacebullying.org/2017-us-survey/.

Chapter 20

1. Susan Heathfield, "Open Door Policy," The Balance Careers, November 23, 2019, https://www.thebalancecareers.com/open-door-policy-1918203.

Chapter 22

1. William Griffith Wilson, also known as Bill Wilson or Bill W., was the cofounder of Alcoholics Anonymous.

Chapter 23

1. Tom Rabe tweet, July 25, 2018, https://twitter.com/Rabe9/status/1022286959572443136.

Chapter 27

1. Tim Ferris, *The 4-Hour Workweek*, https://fourhourworkweek.com/.

Section 3

1. John Kotter, "What Leaders Really Do," *Harvard Business Review*, December 2001, https://hbr.org/2001/12/what-leaders-really-do.

Chapter 28

1. Gene Hammett, "Overprotecting Your Team Members Puts Them at Risk. Do This Instead," *Inc.*, September 19, 2018, https://www.inc.com/gene-hammett/you-need-to-stop-bubble-wrapping-your-team-do-this-instead.html.

Chapter 29

1. Steve Jobs, Cofounder, Chairman, and CEO of Apple Inc., quoted in Tony Siesfeld, Jacquelyn Cefola, and Dale Neef, *The Economic Impact of Knowledge* (Routledge, 1998), 159.

Chapter 31

1. U.S. Department of Labor, May 24, 2018, https://www.dol.gov /odep/topics/SAW-RTW/docs/FOA-ODEP-18-01-Published-on -Grants.gov.pdf.

Chapter 32

1. Ingrid Vaughan, Leadership Academy, January 2020, https://www .smart-hr.ca/workshops-2.

Chapter 33

1. "A Modern Tale of Witnesses Doing Nothing, Except When . . ." Workplace Bullying Institute.

2. Gary Namie, PhD, "Results In: 2017 WBI U.S. Workplace Bullying Survey."

Chapter 35

1. Meghan Casserly, "True Stories from the Holiday Party Files," *Forbes*, December 2, 2010, https://www.forbes.com/sites/meghancasserly /2010/12/02/holiday-office-party-bad-behavior/#5e5601ac303b.

Chapter 36

1. Suzanne Lucas, "Someone Hacked My LinkedIn Account," *Inc.*, October 2, 2017, https://www.inc.com/suzanne-lucas/someone -sabotaged-my-linkedin-account.html.

Chapter 37

1. Eric Rosenbaum, "IBM artificial intelligence can predict with 95 percent accuracy which workers are about to quit their jobs," CNBC, April 3, 2019, https://www.cnbc.com/2019/04/03/ibm-ai-can-predict-with-95-percent-accuracy-which-employees-will-quit.html.

Acknowledgments

1. Eric C. Hansen and Ron A. Carucci, *Rising to Power: The Journey of Exceptional Executives* (Austin, TX: Greenleaf Book Group, 2014), https://www.navalent.com/resources/books/rising-to-power/.

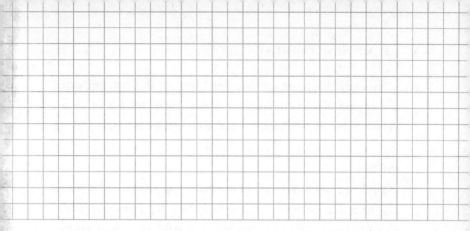

Acknowledgments

I am grateful to all the people who contributed stories or anecdotes about poor management: either their own, or those inflicted upon them. Many of you asked for anonymity and I will respect that wish here, but you know who you are and how valuable your input was in ensuring this book was grounded in reality.

My special thanks to an extraordinary young woman, Megan Shaw-MacDonald. Without your support in researching and developing many of the stories in this book, I doubt I would have made my publishing deadline. Your research, editing, and writing skills helped make this book what it is, and I am proud that you chose me as a mentor.

To Ingrid Vaughan, my longtime friend, confidante, supporter, and awesome human resources specialist: Thank you for such wonderful stories of mismanagement. Your clients at Smart HR are lucky to have such a dedicated, caring individual looking after their HR needs.

Special thanks to Ron Carucci, managing partner of Navalent, and bestselling author of *Rising to Power: The Journey of Exceptional Executives*,[1] for providing the wonderful story about passive-aggressive management.

To Hjalmar Gislason, the founder and CEO of GRID, a SaaS (software as a service) business in Iceland, your excellent contribution to the chapter on managers who talk too much was honest, refreshing, and insightful.

I'd also like to thank the following people who kindly sent me stories: Timothy Wiedman (associate professor, Doane University), Anthony Babbitt (Babbitt Family Foundation), Neill Marshall (Marshall Koll & Associates), and Jacob Dayan (Community Tax, LLC).

Finally, I'd like to thank my wife, Sheila, who is always there for me when I'm pulling my hair out over a paragraph that I can't seem to get right, or when the light at the end of the tunnel turns out to be an oncoming train.

—Mike Wicks (January 2020)